AL PHABET SOUP FOR GR

26 Ways to Not Worry (Really!), Be Happy (Truly!), and Get Over Yourself (Finally!)

Anthony Meindl

Illustrations by Steve Bermundo

ALPHABET SOUP FOR GROWN-UPS: 26 Ways to Not Worry (Really!), Be Happy (Truly!), and Get Over Yourself (Finally!)

Edited by: Sharon Blynn

Illustrations by: Steve Bermundo

Published by:

Meta Creative

7817 Melrose Ave, Los Angeles, CA 90046

www.anthonymeindl.com

ISBN-13: 9780615863689

ISBN-10: 061586368X

Printed in the United States of America

TABLE OF CONTENTS

AN INTRODUCTION

When I thought about writing a second book, I wasn't sure I had another book in me and was daunted by how I could cover new ground that wasn't necessarily examined in *At Left Brain Turn Right*.

A friend of mine gave me the idea, telling me it should be a compilation of my YouTube video lectures. That idea intrigued me, since the vlogs are generally brief (under 7 minutes), and are new explorations of dynamics that interest me in human nature: how to get out of our own way, how to live a more joyful and creative life, how to judge ourselves less and live more passionately now.

Those ideas have been the thrust of my teachings and I've discovered that living a spiritual life — which is simply living a life of courage and honesty, compassion and self-expression — is sometimes given a much more complex explanation than it really needs. And in so doing, we often feel we're spiritual failures. Or others are more "evolved" than we are. Or that we're never going to "make it."

That couldn't be further from the truth. Those ideas just comprise another set of academic, cerebral conceits that keep us from discovering and living the spiritual (and ultimate artistic) expression of self in our daily lives.

So I set myself the task of distilling sometimes highly intellectual, philosophical and scientific concepts into very short chapters all under separate letters of the alphabet. While at the same time wanting to subvert this *idea* that spirituality, creativity and our self-growth have to always be painful, angst-ridden and oh, so *serioso!*

I took my inspiration from Edward Gorey's *The Gashlycrumb Tinies*, which is an abecedarian book from the '60s. Its dark humor tells the tale of 26 children (whose names each represent a letter of the alphabet) coming to their . . . ummmm . . . untimely and sometimes gruesome deaths, all accompanied by rhymed couplets and illustrations. I always felt badly for "U is for Una who slipped down a drain. V is for Victor squashed under a train."[1] Ouch.

So what follows is a tiny homage to Mr. Gorey (in a way). It's not nearly so— errrr . . . gory, but I think it captures the essence of what interesting art (and science) is all about: it's not always reducible to one thing, one explanation, one definition. It's something at times untested and non-traditional; an attempt at exploring and expressing new forms or styles that can easily be understood for the new times we're living in. Or, as Mr. Gorey himself once said, "Ideally, if anything were any good, it would be indescribable."[2]

A

ASK different questions
if you want a new life,
or what you'll end up with
are days filled with strife.

I had a stunning realization recently. (No, not that I look like Aaron Eckhart on a good day. Sigh. And on a bad day . . . Mr. Burns from *The Simpsons*!) I'm talking about the kind of epiphany that comes when we discover that life is so much more than our minds tell us. Or actually, our lives are *exactly* what our minds tell us. It's not mind over matter. It's mind *into* matter.

Our expectations in life (and therefore, *experiences*) are a direct result of the questions we ask ourselves on a daily basis. When we ask questions from our brain's ingrained neural grooves (simply, thought patterns formed by frequent, habitual use), we don't have access to the things we really desire in life. So repetitively asking, "Why am I so fat?" "Could I be any uglier?" "Why would they choose me, stupid?" "Why's it always so hard?" "Why can't I ever get ahead?" "Will it ever happen for me?" "Why am I so f***ed up?" puts us sort of right back where we started.

Well, that sucks!

Our experiences in life then support those limiting beliefs that further reinforce our brains' neural grooves that keep us stuck. So a vicious cycle is created that's hard to escape from and we rarely have access to the answers we seek. Instead, we just get more of the same. More challenges. More missed opportunities. More struggles. More dissatisfaction. More disappointments.

I want a *new* neural groove, dammit!

Unfortunately, we can't just go to the corner garage and ask for a trade-in.

But what we *can* do for an upgrade is start asking different questions that engage us in the world in a new way. We can ask questions that excite us. That break old patterns. That get us thinking along a new groove. Psychologists say it takes anywhere from 21 to 30 days to establish new patterns in our brain. So why not ask questions that create hope, possibility, and passion within us and force us to get activated in the world?

Instead of, "Why me?" what if you asked, "How can I make a difference?"

"Who me?" Yes, you.

Instead of, "Who am I to do that?" try, "How can I best share my unique gifts with the world?"

"You mean I have some?"

Duh.

No more, "Why doesn't it ever happen for me?" when you could be saying, "What can I do to positively inspire more people?"

Share more.

"How can I have more fun?"

Make a conscious *choice* to do so.

"Have more love?"

Give more love.

"Feel more empowered in everything I do?"

Believe that you are empowered. Because you are. A lot more than you realize.

Asking those kinds of questions immediately begins to change us. Changes how we feel about ourselves. Changes what we think is possible. And changes how we perceive the world and how we interact with it.

Sometimes I encourage people to simply "Fake it until they make it." It may seem weird at first. But if we start to really *fake*-believe our way into something, eventually that shadow of a belief will start to become real. And there's science now to prove it. For example, our body will produce good-feeling hormones and reduce our stress hormone (cortisol) when we assume certain body positions that make us feel empowered, even if we don't *feel* empowered.

Nobody has really gotten anywhere in life without a little bit of faking it. Without a little bit of vamping until they figure it out. That's because *no one* has it all figured out. We figure it out as we move along. Just ask Michael Phelps. Or Yo-Yo Ma. Or Hillary Clinton. Or Ryan Gosling. Or Katie Couric. Or Justin Bieber!

So keep asking better questions, like, "If someone can scale Mt. Everest, then why can't I?" "If she can design a new popular iPhone App, then why can't I?" "If he can write a hit song, then why can't I?" "If Honey Boo Boo can have a TV show, then why can't I?"

And as we discover the answer — "Damn right, I can!" — we'll also start to believe that the fake-believe questions we're posing will not only deliver real answers but that those answers are reachable. Doable. Achievable.

Real beliefs will be forged from asking different questions (even if you have to fake them at first), and create new neural grooves.

So it all begins with posing questions.

Just make sure you're asking the right ones.

B

BE more like Scooby-Doo... Be, Do...
And what you'll discover is
it's all about you.

Little did I know as a kid, that the scaredy-cat—errr . . . *dog*, Scooby-Doo, was actually like a badass Buddhist monk. I was too busy trying to tie my own orange ascot like his-hotness-but-blandness Fred and fantasizing about him getting it on with sexy, danger-prone Daphne in her Mystery Machine (which she'd occasionally let Fred drive because she wanted to get in his pants!). Obviously, my budding sexuality and vivid imagination (even with cartoon characters) kept me from noticing Scooby (and Velma . . . *yawn*) and the Zen-like teachings of the show.

Like Scooby running from monsters yet trying to solve great mysteries, we too live in the world of action. If you want to get rid of the ghosts, you have to enter the house. If you have great intentions but sit around on your couch all day eating deep-fried Mars bars and watching '70s cartoons (like *Scooby-Doo!*), it ain't gonna happen. Plus, you'll have to do 50 more kettle bell swings and 50 more burpees for your deep-fried regression.

Doing means converting possibility into actuality.

But what gives rise to possibility?

Possibilities are born in a place beyond doing, beyond action. They occur in moments of *being*. Like meditating. As physicist Dr. Amit Goswami says, "In between doing . . . possibilities grow and grow and grow and grow. If there are more possibilities to choose from, my chance of choosing the correct possibility that will answer my problem is better."[3]

So it's not like Judi Dench going apeshit in *Notes on a Scandal*, screaming to Cate Blanchett, "Do! Do! Do! Do! Do!"[4] (She obviously was dealing with *lots* of pent up sexual frustration.)

But it's also not only about *being*. It's not chilling out in a cave in the Himalayas for 10 years and letting your hair grow really long, Rastafarian-style, wearing a loin cloth, and smelling like a ripe gym bunny.

It's what Dr. Goswami calls "Do. Be. Do. Be. Do."[5]

We're taught how to *do* in our culture. How to go after what we want. To be aggressive. To win. (*Swing to the left, swing to the right. Stand up, sit down. Fight, fight, fight!*) But we're not taught that finding a silent space within us actually connects us to the quantum (the stuff from which possibilities originate) and maximizes our potential *to* create. So we can actually "win" more often without anyone else having to lose, because it's about tapping into our own potential. And that's not competitive. That's possibility.

So try to find moments in your life as a daily practice to just *Be*.

I mentioned meditating earlier. Visualize. Go for a walk. Dance. Write. Listen to music. Spend time in Nature. Do yoga. Disconnect from the Virtual Grid (turn off that phone!) and get connected to the Infinite Potential Grid. We're virtually "connected" all the time, but really lack *connection*. Especially with ourselves.

For five minutes every day, find a way to connect with yourself. Make it part of your lifestyle. Watch what happens. You'll start to take your *being* out into the world in a whole new *doing* way.

And you'll begin to solve some great mysteries. Some, even, of the Scooby-Doo variety. Conquering our "ghosts" of negative self-judgments. Exorcising our "demons" that beat us up and feed our self-hatred. Letting go of the "goblins" of our left brains that keep us locked in to fear and anxiety.

And then you'll be humming the chorus.

Scooby-Dooby-Doo, Where Are You?
We got some work to do now
Scooby-Dooby-Doo, Where Are You?
We need some help from you now
You know we got a mystery to solve
So Scooby-Doo, be ready for your act
Don't hold back!
And Scooby-Doo if you come through
You're going to have yourself a Scooby snack!
That's a fact![6]

Indeed. That snack, though, is more like a feast. As we slay these ghoulish beasts, we'll be left to uncover the purer mysteries of the heart. Those that often require patience and self-awareness to uncover. Those that reveal themselves in the silence of solitude, but then burst noisily in our brains like creative light bulb explosions. An

"Aha!" moment giving us clarity we've never had before, helping us to uncover the mysteries of who we are and perhaps why we are.

As human beings *and* human doings.

C

COMMITMENT-phobic is not the best trait.
You'll wake up one day
and find you're too late!

Commitment-phobe. I am one.

There, I said it.

My friend Angela, whom I kindly refer to as Miss Know-It-All, says that when I sexually objectify a potential boyfriend before I've gotten to know him (which is just fancy talk for sleeping with him on the first date!), I then keep myself from having to form intimate bonds with him beyond the sexual.

"What's wrong with that?" I exclaim.

Miss Know-It-All glares at me. "Then stop complaining you don't have a boyfriend."

Ouch. Busted. She has a point.

Is it that if I commit to one person, I'm going to lose my independence? Is it because I'm scared of vulnerability and exposing myself deeply to another? Or is it simply I'm a chickenshit?

Or maybe in the act of commitment to something (or someone), all of our stuff is destined to confront us, making it seem as if the universe is conspiring against us to make that thing that we're actually wanting to see happen . . . *not* happen.

"See what occurs when we commit? All hell breaks loose. So why bother?"

Exactly. And a lot of times, people do stop. They give up. (Or they sleep with someone on the first date.) If something they want doesn't transpire, they see it as a "sign" that it's not the right time. Or it's not supposed to happen. Or that they should try something else. Or that if this is what they really were meant to be doing, it'd be easier.

In this age of new consciousness, people "meta-philosophize" their way out of lots of things. We sometimes use our newly found spirituality as an excuse to not stay in the game. "It's so hard it must be a sign from the universe that I shouldn't be doing this." Or, "The universe is telling me now's not the right time." Or, "There must be a better plan in store for me or it would've worked out."

But what if it were just the opposite? When we passionately commit to something with extraordinary action, we usher into motion a whole cause-and-effect universe that puts things into play that actually aid and assist us on our journey. But we have to be brave enough to continue pushing through to the end. We have to stay the course. Even if the course, in the short term, is full of potholes, obstacles, barbed wire, mine fields, and alligator-filled swamps.

The things that happen to us in life aren't meant to stop us. Some people think they're meant to test our resolve. To test just how committed we truly are.

Maybe.

But what if it were simply the law of physics (both of the quantum and meta variety). That the more we get into the game of life and the more we take action, the more we're going to affect — and be affected by — events.

Some of this is at the thought (or causal) level. All thought has an energy equivalent we send into the universe, and thoughts as energy waves take on material form. Part of our work, then, is to become more mindful of what we're focusing on, thinking about, and exerting energy toward. When we start to take responsibility for *how* we create, we begin to see the ramifications of *what* we create.

But also, part of this is Newtonian Law: "For every action there is an equal and opposite reaction." Which simply means, things are going to happen to us when we're in the world. Our mere physical existence exerts forces that generate the same amount of force back. Actions and forces, then, become "conversations" — i.e., there is no such thing as an action or force that is one-directional. Action begets action, force begets force. Movement begets movement.

So what if we saw our life occurrences in a new context? When things happen to us it means we're activated. We're engaging with the world. We're actually participating *fully* in our lives. All of it. Not just the easy stuff. Not just when things are going well. But the other stuff, too. The experiences that test us or make us feel doubt or feel like a setback.

All. Of. It.

Life's not supposed to be trouble-free. How boring would that be? There'd be no challenge. And we're hard-wired to seek challenge. Challenges are what lead us to develop curiosity and insight. They foster adventures and ask us to problem solve. Challenges reveal latent talents within us. They demonstrate our strength of character. Our malleability. Our sense of humor. Our resilience. Our spirit.

There's no force out there trying to keep us from what we want. There's no evil troll in the sky throwing curve balls at us, gleefully responding, "Muhaha! You cannot have this!"

The universe is neutral (*Thank Gawd!*). It doesn't impose. And why should it? The only thing keeping you from what you want is this: You're not *committing* to what you want. Period.

Yikes.

Well, that's sort of a slap in the face and brings us back to Miss Know-It-All.

You mean, I might be able to get what I want if I changed my behavior and committed to the long-term picture of what I wish to see happen and not the short-term goal of having my sexual fantasies fulfilled after a chocolate-infused café-au-lait with my dream date and asking what his astrological sign is (a *Leo!*) before we hightail it out of there, riding in his eco-friendly Nissan Leaf to Lover's Lane Lookout?

Yep.

D

DRAMA. Does it always have to be so... dramatic?
Well, duh, yes, as we like our
lives to be very cinematic!
(Cue soundtrack for the movie Titanic!)

L isten up, Drama Queens! Yes, that's you.

Let's get one thing straight: drama is our *story* about conflict. And yes, some of those stories are *fascinating*, like Cheyenne on *Bridalplasty* saying such memorable things as, "Dr. Dubrow can fix faces . . . he can't fix personalities."[7]

Indeed.

But what if we understood conflict from a quantum perspective, gaining a new awareness of how to use conflict when it arises in a way that's healthy and creative?

"You mean throwing plates at my ex and keying her car isn't healthy?" Well, I'll give you style points for being creative! Healthy? Not so much.

If you examine your life, the periods of greatest conflict were also the opportunities for greatest growth and awareness. You were stressed about a job, had an argument with your spouse, or decided to take a risk to do something new. These situations were either fueled by inner conflict with yourself (*I'm stupid. No I'm not. Yes I am. No I'm not!*) or outer conflict with another (*I hate you. No you don't. Yes I do!*). But by staying *in* the conflict — not running away, not shutting down, not ignoring it — you got to the other side.

Resolution was created, and with that came possibility. Access to something new and undiscovered. Potential. An "Aha!" moment. Creativity. Healing. Insight. Peace. Make-up sex. A trip to Magic Mountain. Courtside Laker's tickets. Frozen yogurt!

But we often bail when things get crunchy before we experience the positive results that are born through conflict. Why do we avoid it? Well, duh, it sucks. But there are a few other reasons.

1) We're not taught how to be *conscious* in conflict, so it shuts us down. ("You mean turning up the TV volume really loud and downing a bottle of Jack Daniel's when my girlfriend's yelling at me isn't conscious?") Clever, yes. Conscious, no.

2) We let it defeat us. We give up. We quit. We don't realize conflict is not only okay, but is also essential in our transformation and growth. ("Are you calling me a quitter?" Well, kind of . . . Sort of . . . Don't hurt me.)

3) We misinterpret it. We think just because there's conflict in our lives that there must be something wrong with us. Or we're a failure. Or other people don't have conflict. (It sucks when we compare ourselves to the celebrities of the world. First, they have perfect hair. Second, they can just pay someone to have conflict for them!)

Or so we think.

But if life were devoid of conflict, there would be no opportunity for evolution. We would exist in a state of nothingness. Homeostasis. Stagnation. From a biological standpoint, all species evolution has occurred through the triumphing over conflict to adapt. It's called Natural Selection.

It's *natural.*

And like it or not, *we* were selected. So get over it. Well, not really "selected" but more an ever-evolving end product of evolutionary adaptation . . . but natural, yes. (Although, Miss Clairol, your hair color may not be.)

It's what evolved us from a quadruped to a biped. And that's just fancy talk for our originating from prokaryotic bacteria (aka sludge) into the amazing, bacteria-squeamish, hand-sanitizing addicts we now are. Pass the Purell!

Stop confusing conflict with drama. Stop making conflict so scary. Stop making it bad.

Conflict is just a part of life's process to spur us on to our next level.

We're all eventually going to get there. We can go kicking and screaming and having a hissy fit and then telling everyone about it like Regina George did in *Mean Girls* . . .

"Like this one time, I got this really expensive dollhouse from Germany, but I never played with it. So my mom wanted to give it to my cousin. But even though I didn't want it . . . I threw it down the stairs. I didn't want anyone else to have it. But that's just me." [8]

Well, Regina, that's one way.

Or, we can talk about it less. Resolve it more.

So the next time you want to hurl your favorite Scandinavian-inspired dollhouse down the stairs, maybe you redesign it as an eco-friendly, environmentally-green duplex instead. And share it with your neighbor.

Resolution.

Good for you. And good for the planet.

E

EMOTIONAL Zombies
are not just on TV.
When we don't want to feel —
they're inside all of us,
including you and me.

Take the Zombie challenge.

Do you kill a lot of time watching YouTube cat videos? (And who doesn't?) Refreshing your Twitter feed every 30 seconds? Watching *Zombie Prom* again and again? Staring at your own reflection in your gym's mirror more often than you look at your girlfriend? Then it's time for an intervention!

You're a zombie.

But don't dismay. Zombies are all the rage right now! Zombies are *in*. The problem is, zombies don't feel. That's what makes them—errr . . . zombies. But as human beings, the conduit through which we express is feeling.

But it's often hard to access deep feeling when our lives become a defensive gesture in order to survive. We develop a thick armor around us as a means of self-preservation. I get it. If you've been made fun of for being who you are, you become less secure in wanting to share who you are with people. If you've been dumped when your heart seems the most open, you become less willing to open your heart to someone again.

As we feel things and then hurt, we often retreat in the direction of safety, comfort, emotional stasis. We avoid anything that makes us feel vulnerable or exposed.

But in the avoidance of these feelings that scare us, we end up *anesthetizing* ourselves. We become emotionally comatose.

"Doctor! Doctor! Get the defibrillator, stat! I can't feel a pulse!"

"Well, nurse, that's because you're giving mouth-to-mouth to a zombie!"

Yuk.

We become emotional zombies in our own lives. And unless we're going to Central Casting for a role on *The Walking Dead*, being a zombie is *never* a good thing.

The *science of feeling* is to understand that no feeling exists *outside* of the whole. In order to feel anything — including bliss and ecstasy and really feeling *alive* — you have to allow yourself to feel *all* feeling, including the stuff you don't like. They're all parts of the same whole. To disallow one thing is to cut yourself off from something else.

Stop running away from the thing you dread and just feel it instead. You'll see that by allowing yourself to actually *feel* — even if that feeling sucks temporarily — you'll be more alive, more present, more available than you've possibly been in a long time. And you'll actually see that the thing you were so scared of feeling is not that big a deal.

We're *feeling* beings.

Stop thinking your way through life and start feeling your way through it. And for goodness sakes, get off the zombie train. They're not nearly as cool as we think they are. And like most things with a designated shelf life (bandana headbands, low-rise jeans, *Teletubbies*, flash mobs!), they'll no longer be "in" by 2015 or so.

You heard it here first, folks. It's a lot more fun to be alive than it is to be undead.

F

FUCK IT!
Sometimes it's what you need.
Doing it for yourself is really what helps you succeed.

W hy do we care so much what others think of us? Is it because we all suffer from some sort of arrested development and are trying to overcome our collective low self-esteem generated by our "awkward phase" in adolescence? Will we ever escape high school and our desire to be voted "Most Popular"?

I'm not sure we ever fully get off the teenage scary-go-'round of wanting to be liked. Or wishing we were more attractive, more "cool", more "in".

Say it isn't so, Tony!

"You like me . . . Right now . . . You like me!" screamed Sally Field in 1985 after winning her Oscar.[9]

Ummm . . . she was 34! That's 16 years *after* high school!

I rest my case.

Except for you sick puppies who actually seemed to *enjoy* the smell of those bleach-mopped hallways, for most of us, high school was a trial-by-fire experience of figuring out who we were, learning how to become independent, hiding from people who'd hurt us, trying to keep food from getting stuck in our braces, and pretty much living in a constant state of low-level panic.

Sort of like . . . well . . . starring in our own high school version of the movie *Carrie*.

So at one level, because what everyone struggles with as adults are the same core issues that high school traumas brought up for us (like surviving lunch period!), we often revert to our teenage paradigms of how we see ourselves: we're not good enough or we're inadequate or flawed in some way; we're not worthy or desirable; we're weird or unlovable. The outcast. The nerd. The freak.

Well, even though at 16 I thought I was the only one feeling vulnerable (yet fashionable!) in my pleated madras shorts and pink Izod shirt, what I discovered later is that what we're feeling is what *everyone* is feeling.

When we apply for a job or have an interview or go into an audition room, we incorrectly think we're the only one who feels insecure. News flash: everyone in the room does. We all have the same vulnerabilities. It may seem like the people making the decisions have the power, but we're all on equal footing here. At a business level, they need us as much as we need them. And at a core human level, everyone wants to be liked and understood. Everyone wants to be seen and heard. Everyone is trying to do their best.

And just like we want the casting director or the gallery owner or the business manager to like us and our work, they want people to like *them*. (Or at least not fire them.) They answer to a producer or HR person or a district manager who is in turn answering to a director or hiring administrator or vice president who ultimately might be answering to a corporation that owns the world. Like GE.

You get the idea.

Become more internally referenced. You're never going to get out of that high school lunchroom if you keep looking outside yourself for the answers, the confirmation, the support, the love, or the appreciation. First of all, "out there" is a reflection of "in here". So what we're seeking out there is something we aren't fulfilling for ourselves, inside.

People are fickle. Why? Because we're all externally referenced. Judgments are made by the last job we had, how we look or how skinny we are, how much money we make, how young or hot we are, who we know, or what kind of shoes we're wearing. (They're Kenneth Cole, by the way.) But those things change. We're on top today; tomorrow we're fired. Our show's #1 this week; then it's cancelled. We drive a Mercedes now; next month, a used Yugo.

If your identity is based on the external, what happens when the externals are taken away? *Eeeek.* "I don't know who I am when I look in the mirror!" Well, I do. Someone who doesn't know who they are.

If you're waiting to hear it from your husband, or your teacher, or your lover; your coach, your mother, your best friend, your kids, your peers — it's possible you may never hear it. Or what you do hear won't be enough. Or it won't be said the way you want to hear it.

You have to give this to yourself first.

Stop trying to impress *them*. You can't. You won't. Why? Because "them" — the people you are so obsessed with trying to get to like you — aren't really thinking about you.

What?

I'll repeat it for emphasis. *They're. Not. Thinking. About. You.*

Because who they're thinking about is . . . high school marching band drumroll, please . . . *Themselves!* Like each of us, on a daily basis, the person we're most concerned about is . . . Sarah Palin. No, it's not. It's *you*. (And who's Sarah Palin most concerned about? Herself. Oh, and the Russians.) We think about people vis-à-vis our own needs, desires, anxieties, goals, hopes, dreams, fears, and situations. Just like everyone does.

We share one world here, but there are also 7 billion micro-worlds occurring within one world. We share the same consciousness, but at the same time, there are 7 billion experiences of individual ego consciousness happening simultaneously.

Think about it. Look back in your address book at the people who seemed so important to you five years ago. Some of them may still be in your life. But all of them? Probably not.

Where's that *amazing* guy ("He's the one!") you tried to impress in your Forever 21 outfit? He's now doing time in the Ohio Federal Penitentiary. (Perhaps you've become pen pals?) Where's that retail manager you did a song-and-dance for to get him to hire you? He's now a taxidermist specializing in pigeon poses. Where's the "expert" who told you that you lacked talent? He's shoveling guinea pig shit at the Palmdale Petco. (Nothing wrong with guinea pigs . . . I love them. And Petco seems like a groovy place to work if you're an animal lover.) The point is these people are *not* the boss of you.

Work toward doing it for you. Work toward applauding you. Work toward the validation and acceptance and love and support coming from you. Ironically, when you do that, you'll begin to see it starting to show up more often in your *external* world.

If other people give it to us — well golly! — that's a nice bonus (sort of like when flight attendants give us *two* packets of roasted peanuts on a 7-hour flight). If they don't, it won't be the end of the world. (But we will be *really* hungry and cranky!) Because the true victories in life are in conquering the noise in our heads that takes us back to high school lunchroom periods over and over again.

Remember this the next time you do it for anyone but yourself. Cast out those doubts placed in your head by that 7th grade bully. Wrestle to the ground those fears of failure shouted at you by your 9th grade wrestling coach. Give yourself your own title of Prom King or Prom Queen stolen by your senior nemesis.

It simply doesn't matter what anyone else says or thinks of you. What they think of you is none of *your* business. Their limitations of you are *their* limitations.

So . . . remember to say "Fuck It!"

And listen as you begin to hear yourself saying, "I love myself . . . Right now . . . I love myself."

G

GOAT.
You have one (we all do).
Now sell it! Get rid of it before "it" becomes two.

We don't have to be a sheepherder in Outer Mongolia or trade that piglet we've got on our family farm for a Holstein cow. It's a metaphor.

We've all got goats. Some of them seem cute and cuddly, like those cheeky marionettes from "The Lonely Goatherd" in *The Sound of Music*. Others are mean and do a lot of ramming.

In her book, *Living Your Yoga*, Judith Lasater, recounts an old Yiddish folktale about "selling the goat," which is about making a stressful situation (like standing in line at the DMV or anything involving clowns) better by stepping away and looking at it with a new pair of eyes (or bifocals for some of us). She decided to make the moral of the story into a Mantra for Daily Living, encouraging readers to, when in troublesome scenarios, "inhale gently, and on your next exhalation, say to yourself 'Sell the goat.'"[8]

Breathe. And try to let go of our fixed, fearful hold on things, seeing the situation from a more accurate perspective.

I'm taking her idea one step further. To me, "the goat" represents not only our conditioned way of interpreting things and our habituated response from a negative, limited-view way of thinking, but also, it represents the multitude of distractions in our lives.

You know the ones. Unsupportive friends. (They who smile in your company but behind your back cut you with a dull butter knife.) Negative lovers. (The ones who say, "You're going to wear *that?*") Disrespectful agents. (You call and the assistant says, "Sorry, he's out to lunch." But it's only 10 a.m.!) Toxic relationships. (Your boyfriend needs you to pay his rent *again* this month, but promises this is the *last time*.) Two-timing partners. ("No. My name is *not* Susan!") Mean managers. (I once had a manager tell me I did weird things with my mouth. Well, of course I was doing weird things with my mouth . . . I was *singing a song* at the time!)

Sell it.

Get rid of it.

Dump it.

Drop it.

Buh-bye it.

Email and *au revoir* it!

Life's too short.

We end up expending so much energy on things that don't hasten our growth, or nurture our talent, but instead make us question and doubt ourselves (i.e., we create unnecessary drama! See *"'D' as in Drama"* chapter). We attract people to ourselves who make us feel unworthy and untalented, and who support our incorrect belief that we don't deserve any better. (And Lord knows, we get that in spades from our family, God love 'em, who are a lot harder to drop, so why in Toledo would we want others like this in our life?)

When distracted by such energy-suckers, make this your new mantra: "I don't have that kind of time."

We don't, people. No one does. Except for maybe those kooky kids from *Twilight*. They're immortal!

So, simply. Effortlessly. Sell. The. Goat.

Your farm will become a lot more manageable. And you might discover you've been lactose-intolerant all this time. *That* explains all that painful gas, lethargy, and malaise. Watch how much lighter, more energized, and less bloated you'll be.

(As an added incentive, with each figurative goat we sell, buy a literal goat for someone who really needs it. Go to www.Heifer.org and take the money we're saving by no longer paying for our girlfriend's student loans while she's shacking up with our best friend in Puerto Vallarta and instead do something positive. Our donation helps farmers in developing countries to provide for their families, and sometimes whole villages, by purchasing a goat or cow or water buffalo that ensures ending hunger and helps people overcome poverty.)

So selling our goat (or literally buying one!) can change us *and* the world.

One goat at a time.

H

HOW to Train Your Dragon...
won't win you a gold medallion,
but it might just set you free.

Not unlike the DreamWorks movie, if you want to make your Dragon work for you, you first have to know you have one. Or a hundred. And then learn how to tame them.

Once upon a time, we were given a travel companion, our Ego Dragon, to help us navigate through life's travails. Our Ego Dragon processed information, evaluated situations, made judgments based on experiences, remembered the past, and made plans.

It had a useful purpose. It helped shape our identity and carried us through the world avoiding things that it perceived as dangerous and unknown. ("Tony, you're entering a crack den. Leave now!" "Thank you, Dragon. That was scary!")

But as we grew, so did our Dragon. *Feed me! Feed me!* And so we did. We gave it unsubstantiated information based on past experiences. We avoided things that were unknown to us because the Dragon said it was unsafe. We repeated things to ourselves that our Dragon overheard: *You're a freak. You're fat. You're ugly. You're so cool. You're the shit.* (It wasn't his fault. These were things he heard others say — both good *and* bad — so they *had* to be truthful, he thought.)

Our Dragon ended up spawning lots of little Dragons ("He" is actually a "She" *and* a "He" and therefore *very* fertile!), and now we really had our hands full. More than three thousand years ago, the Bhagavad Gita portion of the longest poem ever written, the *Mahabharata*, stated that we have 100 formidable Dragons. Scary. And all of them will fight us on the battlefield of man's body.

That's a lot of freakin' Dragons!

Now if you had 100 little baby Dragons to tend to — what would your life be spent doing?

No, not taking over make-believe kingdoms and freeing slaves like Daenerys Targaryen does with her 3 Dragons in *Game of Thrones*. (And she has her hands full with just 3!)

Mostly, it'd be comprised of figuratively feeding all your little Dragons; that is, maintaining and defending untruths that seemed real. Somewhere around page 897 of the *Mahabharata*, we're reminded of the Dragons we have to fight within ourselves. And everywhere we look, we're confronted by them.

We walk around aimlessly (Dragon), lost (Dragon), and confused (Dragon), and feeling sorry for ourselves (Dragon). Sort of how Mel Gibson (*DRAGON!!!*) must have felt after being pulled over by a female cop. "What do you think you're looking at, sugar tits?"[10] *Ummmm . . . Mel, you're in desperate need of Dragon-slaying.*

Or how about that lovely Miss Teen USA contestant from South Carolina who was stumped by not only Mario Lopez's good looks (and who wouldn't be?), but also by the geography question thrown at her by that cheeky, Miley Cyrus-looking judge. "Recent polls have shown a fifth of Americans can't locate the US on a world map. Why do you think this is?"[11]

Well, I would have said, "Because they're too busy making their own music videos of Carly Rae Jepson's 'Call Me Maybe'"!

But she didn't.

"I personally believe, that, U.S. Americans are unable to do so because . . . uh . . . some people out there in our nation don't have maps and . . . uh . . . I believe that our education — like such as in South Africa and the Iraq (everywhere like, such as, and) — I believe that they should . . . our education over here in the U.S. should help the U.S. — or should help South Africa — and should help the Iraq and Asian countries, so we will be able to build up our future for our children."[12]

Take that, Miss Texas!

Now you might be thinking, you lost me at, "everywhere like, such as . . . and U.S. Americans." (Can someone say redundant?) But, like Miss South Carolina, we, too, let our nerves get the best of us. We, too, feel inadequate. Unprepared. Not capable. Out of our league. Unworthy. Inarticulate. And it does sometimes feel like trying to find our way back on a very foreign map in "the Iraq and Asian countries."

And you know what that is? *No, not South Africa.* Ego. Yes, the Ego Dragon of nerves, self-consciousness, compare-and-despair-ism, low self-esteem, and negative self-judgments.

But wait, Ginsu knife lovers . . . there's more.

Training to be in *any* kind of beauty pageant must be hard (especially for those toddlers in tiaras). As any contestant knows, forget the inner, you have to perfect the outer. *That hair! That smile! That walk!* So you go to pageant boot camp where you not only get toned and buff (and get your spray tan on!) but also get to look really, really hot in your Dragon-slaying outfits.

Like a kick-butt Thor (or Lisbeth in *Girl with the . . .* wait for it . . . *Dragon Tattoo*), through awareness and perseverance (and lots of piercings and eye shadow), we gain insight into a whole other part of ourselves we never knew existed. We're then ready to meet our Dragons on the battlefield. Some, from the Gita, we immediately get rid of: meanness, cruelty, ill will, conceit, pessimism, bitterness. While we negotiate with others that often become habitual: impatience, worry, laziness. (Ah, yes, I know them too well.)

Since time began, the *real* battle every person fights is the battle against the enemies *within*. They are conquerable. They're there to help us cultivate another part of ourselves that is much larger, much grander, and doesn't identify with the ego-based identities we're here to slay.

So thank your Dragons. Without them, we wouldn't be able to experience a different part of ourselves that *transcends* them, and in so doing, reveals to us who we truly are.

So your Dragons are neither good nor bad. But they *can* be dangerous. So for goodness sakes, stop feeding them. Stop letting them run rampant, scorching the earth and your life with their fire-breathing ways. They can be tamed. Don't let their fierce exterior and sometimes scary appearance intimidate you. You are the master. They are here to work for you. Not the other way around.

Oh, and turn in that tiara for a world map soon. You're going to need it to navigate where your Dragon might take you. It's called your life's journey.

I

INFINITE Intelligence.
You're smarter than you know.
A creative, talented adventurer,
just like Jacques Cousteau.

No, not *Artificial Intelligence* for you Comic-Con geeks. *Infinite* Intelligence. Which is just a fancy-schmancy way of saying you're smart. Really, really smart, and you don't know it.

Now you may be thinking, "I didn't feel smart when I had that seventh tequila shot and body slammed the security guard!" Or, "Why did I say yes to tanning with iodine and baby oil?" Or, "I think I just sexted topless photos of myself to my boss! Oops."

You're absolutely right. That's not smart, people . . . that's *dumb*.

But what I'm talking about isn't book smarts, street smarts, or all-around common sense (or epic *fails*). It's an intelligence that transcends left-brain mechanics; an evolutionary hard-wiring that we each innately possess that plugs us into the intuitive knowing of the universe. Connection to it *all*. Even to that which we may not fully grasp.

In the 1970s (though I was just a mere pup), I would sit mesmerized in front of our rabbit-eared TV watching *The Undersea World of Jacques Costeau*. (I *loved* saying his name. *Oui Oui!*) Our fearless, intrepid leader in the red beret and the thick French accent would take us on a thrilling adventure each week, unraveling mysteries of the sea. Back then, I realized the universe was so vast, so unexplored, and so uncharted, I felt small and . . . well . . . dumb in comparison.

But Jacques had this amazing way of making me feel that I was connected to it all; to something bigger than myself, but still a part of it. Something intelligent. Unknown, yet soon-to-be discovered. That we (according to the ominous, *Twilight Zone*-ish opening voice-over of the show) were entering, "once more, the mysterious, dark world that spawned [us] 300 million years ago."[13]

And in those moments I *did* feel connected to something ancient, mysterious, vast.

Physicist Adam Frank talks about four distinct domains of intuitive knowledge with which we are all born that govern language, human psychology, biology, and, believe it or not, physics. He says, "In each of these domains there is evidence that humans evolved with an internal guidebook of understanding, a degree of hard-wiring imprinted by evolution."[14]

Hot damn! We all have an inner Einstein. And it dates back to millions of years ago.

Basically, this evidence suggests that we have access to the infinite organizing power of universal intelligence that governs all existence. It's contained within you. And me. And all forms of life. From a paramecium to a parrot. Indeed all living beings have some sort of consciousness. We all share it. The gift (and sometimes the curse) for *human* beings is that we are aware of our consciousness.

The creative life force of intelligence freely moves through a tulip or jellyfish, let's say, to fulfill their roles in nature in which all things play an integral part. We, however, impede our own connection to this ever-evolving, ever-expanding life force because we incorrectly believe we're smarter than it. So for us humans, our job is to get out of our own way so that this intelligence can move through us.

Intuitively.

And stop seeing ourselves as separate.

Let's break this down old school.

Why don't we get what we want in life?

You know, the hot boyfriend with biceps like Jake Gyllenhaal? The multimillion-dollar record deal? A seat on the bus? A ballad sung to us by Taylor Swift?

Well, we actually *do* get what we want in life, but since we insist that the thing we desire looks the way we *think* it's supposed to look (I asked for Jake Gyllenhaal, dammit!) and because it *never* does, we actually shut out what wants to present itself in our experience (which is *what we want*), and we miss it completely.

How's that?

We ignore it. We deny it. We refuse to see the possibility in it. It wants to show us the way and generate creative ideas, but we think we know better. So we end up with nothing. Or rather, we end up with a lot but it never seems to square away with the *idea* of what we want, so it feels like we're getting squat.

There is our *idea* of life and how we want it to unfold . . . then there's life.

When we give up our ideas (and expectations) of how things are supposed to be and instead embrace what we have, we begin to see some interesting patterns. Patterns of intuitive promptings whispering to us, "This is the way." "Try this." "Don't be scared." "Give it a go." "Trust." "Jake Gyllenhaal is taken anyway . . . move on to Joe Jonas!"

When we start listening to the hunches, an "Aha!," an inner charge, we start to move in the direction of that thing we're wanting, even if we can't see it yet.

And that's when the "Hows" of life become the "Wows". We begin to stop worrying about the "Hows". ("How will I get there?" "How will it work?" "How do I know?" "How is it possible?" "How can I be sure?") We jump in. And by doing so, we get to the other side and see that the "Hows" get taken care of in ways that the left brain's miniscule, controlling dialogues could never have imagined.

Infinite Intelligence always trumps the traps of our left-brain dialogues. When we go on the ride, life takes care of the details. Our free will generates the momentum, but once we take action, there are too many coordinates to control and all we can do is *trust* that something is working for our greater good.

Birds do it. Bees do it. (*No, not that!*) Well, they do *do* that. But I'm talking about a surrender. A flow. A natural inclination and connection to energetically follow the path of least resistance and be guided to do the things they're here to do.

We can't orchestrate the details. We can't demand them (try as we might). All we can do is set forth a clear intention and then go on the adventure. Yes, we try. Yes, we take action. Yes, we meet challenges and push through them. Yes, we refuse to accept defeat. All the while knowing that we're being led exactly how we need to be led, letting things unfold naturally.

Life is a lot like driving at night in the fog. Or in a blinding snowstorm. A few years ago, I was driving from a small town in Bavaria to visit my cousin in Munich. (Hello, Oktoberfest!) On the way there, I encountered a virtual whiteout. Panic. The more I strained to see far ahead of me, the more I became blinded by the snow and engulfed in paralysis as to what to do. Keep going? Turn around? Screw this trip and go someplace warm?

I took a deep breath and instead of straining to see miles down the road, I just kept focusing on this truth: All we really have to do is keep illuminating the next 100 feet in front of us. The rest of the road will unfurl before us as we go. We have no control over the conditions; the bumps along the way, the detours and seemingly winding roads. We don't even have to worry so much about the big picture. That will take shape as we just stay in the present of what each moment brings.

Sure enough, I eventually arrived safely at my destination — although truth be told, the hour-long trip did feel more like *four hours* crawling at a snail's pace, white-knuckling it all the way, listening to bad German polka music and hip-hop remixes of "99 Luftballons" — but when I drove into that beer-lovin' city, the storm had passed and I was greeted with the big picture: a dazzling postcard of a gothic town blanketed in pristine, twinkling white. A beautiful image that still stays with me today and reminds me of what I had to get through to get there.

How?

Wow, indeed.

J

JAWS.
Yes, that scary mechanical shark.
What you have in common with Steven Spielberg isn't a lark.

Y ou're probably thinking, "Yeah, I'm obsessed with extraterrestrials and still refuse to go into the ocean alone at night. *Da-dum, da-dum, da-dum* . . . But that's where the similarities between me and one of the greatest directors of all time end."

It's true, that little whippersnapper made his first feature film at the age of 27. You, meanwhile, celebrated your 27th birthday by moving into your parents' basement to save money and pay off your student loans, while secretly inviting hot girls over when your folks were out enjoying the early-bird special at Denny's.

Don't despair, clever one. This is the stuff that will make for a great story later in your life, as the genesis of success can originate from the most unlikely of places. And as you'll see, you have a lot more in common with the directing Maestro than you think.

When we're on the outside looking in, when we compare ourselves to others, when we listen to the glossy, photoshopped stories the media feed us about people who've "made it", we often feel like there's something wrong with us. We lack what other people have.

Namely, we're scared and we think Steven Spielberg (or Rihanna or J. K. Rowling or Roger Federer) isn't.

That's because what we see are the red carpet movie premieres, and book publishing parties, and tennis championships. We compare our dress rehearsal in life to everyone else's opening night. We don't realize that along the way, each of those creators got beaten up, rejected, denied, and wanted to quit. And yes, many moved back in with their parents — and were petrified.

Did you know that despite the huge success of *Jaws*, the film was nearly shut down due to delays and budget overruns? And Spielberg himself said, "I'm glad I got out of Martha's Vineyard (the location shoot) alive."[15] Of course you didn't know that. You were too busy getting eaten by a gigantic, Hollywood-marketed, blockbuster shark!

Academy Award winner Joaquin Phoenix says this about fear: "I want it to be scary — and it still is. I'm almost 38. I've been acting for 30 years. But I still get nauseous the day before and have weeks of incredible anxiety. They have to put fucking pads in my armpits because I sweat so much that it just drips down my wardrobe. For the first three weeks of shooting, I'm just sweating. It's pure anxiety, and I love it."[16]

Spielberg has a painting in his office called *Boy on a High Dive* in which a boy is crouching at the end of a diving board, looking fretfully over the edge. Spielberg says, "For me that [painting] represents every motion picture just before I commit to directing it. Just that one moment."[17]

In other words, his acknowledgment of his fear (just like Mr. Phoenix's) is *also* his access to freedom.

Even after making 27 films, Mr. Spielberg still faces the same stuff we all face. It's all relative.

It's okay to feel fear (especially when we're swimming in the ocean next to a great white shark!). The goal is to understand that it's actually a necessary step of creativity (and not becoming a fish snack).

All artists struggle with it. Don't think there's something flawed or fucked up or wrong with you because you feel it. When you're on the edge of creating — doing something new, pushing to a higher level, reaching a breakthrough, jumping into unknown territory, taking a risk, being vulnerable, taking a stand, committing in your work — you're supposed to feel things. One of them is fear.

"Feel the fear and do it anyway!" is the saying. Fear is not supposed to stop you. Nor should it when you discover that everyone who creates feels it.

So the next time you're swimming in the middle of the ocean. At night. Alone. Naked. And you hear the echoes of that famous tune (*Da-dum, da-dum*) in your head and freak out . . . *get out of the water!*

But the next time you feel scared right before you're about to give a speech to a thousand people, or have your design collection shown at Fashion Week, or shoot your commercial with Alec Baldwin, remember . . . you're simply feeling what Steven Spielberg is feeling.

And it's okay.

You may peer down from the edge of your diving board and not want to jump because the water seems to be filled with a bunch of man-eating sharks. But just like the movie . . . those sharks *aren't real.* They're just the ones swimming around in your head.

So jump. And what you might find waiting for you is something else you and Steven Spielberg might have in common . . . an Academy Award.

K

KIDS.
That's what we still can be.
Spirited and joyful and present and free.

The science is in.

It all comes down to the moment. Are you in it? Are you here?

Now?

When we are, the brain creates what brilliant Harvard psychologist Shawn Achor calls the "Happiness Advantage". Simply, when we are present to the joy of the moment, we not only turn on *all* the learning centers of our brain, but we also perform better than when the brain is "neutral, negative, or stressed."[18]

And we get stressed for all sorts of silly reasons. Forgetting to post that cool photo on Instagram. Our favorite contestant singing way off-key on *American Idol*. Snooki writing a best-selling book. David Hasselhoff doing commercials for Hot Pockets.

Meanwhile, real stressors (not necessarily who got kicked off this week's *The Bachelor*!) make us take the Left-Brain-Drain-Train (next stop, Desperation City — or Dusseldorf if you're a German fan of "The Hoff") and listen to the negative things we tell ourselves when we get triggered in an emotional way.

So how do we stay plugged in to the creative nerve center that generates the desires we have that feel good? (Like singing a duet with Kelly Clarkson!)

Science calls it the brain. I simply call it, "Choose to feel good." Or another way of thinking about it is to re-connect to our inner child. It leads to the same results.

We're taught in life that happiness comes from getting stuff. Babes. Boats. Bling. That stuff's fine. But that's not the real reason why we create, even though the advertising media machine wants to anesthetize you (remember, zombies!) into thinking it is.

What we want is joy. And actually, we don't even want it. We *are* it.

Joy's not *in* any *thing*. It's already ours. It's who we are. It's our essential nature.

Not pleasure. Not excitement. Not titillation. Not euphoria. Not gratification. Those things rock, but sadly, they're transitory. They come and go with the event (a Notre Dame football game!), or person (a date with Mila Kunis!), or experience (I just won a refrigerator on *The Price Is Right!*) that evoked the feeling. And all of those things are temporal.

But joy is not conditional. It abides within us. Always. Regardless of circumstances.

So how do we tap into our natural state, especially if we didn't know we had one? "You're telling me I'm joyful, Tony, when my wife just left me, my car got impounded, and I'm out of a job?"

Think of it this way. Joy is a baseline state of being that is as real a part of us as our ears or our fingernails. It's like a wavelength or bandwidth that contains *all* other transitory feelings on top of it. It's sort of the reservoir that contains all feeling.

Often, we only connect to superficial feelings on a day-to-day basis that are subject to circumstances or events and their outcome; like pleasure, satisfaction, and gratification. Or their darker cousins: anger, resentment, and annoyance. So we're often masked from the deeper state of being that is alive within us and gives rise to these temporal ebbs and flows.

But we don't have to even worry about getting that deep yet. We can make huge strides in life and, as Mr. Achor reminds us, tap into a Happiness Advantage by simply becoming more mindful of what we're choosing to feel.

When we catch ourselves being upset by something, it's generally not because something bad or tragic or truly upsetting occurred. It's because what happened is counter to what we think *should* be happening and it immediately makes us feel pissed, cranky, sad, defeated, belligerent, jealous, threatened, or douche-y. Take your pick.

As adults, we get so oriented toward the end results, the finish line, the pictures of success we feel pressured to fulfill, that we lose the innate sense of play that abides within us in merely *experiencing* life.

You know who naturally has this advantage?

Children.

They don't hold on to grudges and resentments. They adjust their attitude about defeats and take things less personally. They're engaged with the world not for the spoils but for the *experience*. Their joy is derived from being. Participation.

They commit to the reality of their imaginary micro-worlds (whether it's exploring outer space, or playing Samurai swords on an ancient Japanese battlefield, or pretending they're trapped in the Jurassic period hiding from dinosaurs). They can because they think they can. Or rather, their commitment to what they think they can do is what allows them to do it.

That joyful, child-like spirit of who we are hasn't diminished because we're now approaching 30. (Age is a number and mine is unlisted!) We've gained 10 pounds. (I wear it well. Plus there's this new thing called Spanx.) We can't do a backbend anymore. (Who needs that? I take Pilates now.) We have grey hair (Ummm . . . grey is the new black.) Or fit into our favorite jeans from 1988. (They still fit dammit! I'm just bloated today.)

Our ability to change the way we see the world is — scientifically — available to us. It just requires us to change the paradigms we've become accustomed to using as safety armor, as we get older to move through our world.

As author Marianne Williamson says, "Children aren't bored when they wake up in the morning, because they don't know what's going to happen to them that day. Adults are bored because we *think* we do."[19]

This is a good reminder of how we often preempt the moment because we *think* we know the conclusion to something before we've actually experienced it.

Stay open. Shift your perspective. See events through the innocent eyes of the child that we still are. We'll then experience our own Happiness Advantage and begin to tap into our true state of joy.

Someone once said to the Buddha, "I want happiness." The Buddha responded: "First remove 'I' — that's Ego. Then remove 'want' — that's desire. See now what you are left with."

Happiness.

That's who we truly are.

L

LET go...
Or I'll push you. (That doesn't sound kind.)
But what you're looking for, you'll then surely find.

Nerd alert. When I was a kid growing up in Indiana, I'd spend my summers collecting live bugs. There were acres of woods and empty fields behind my house full of more insects than you could swallow on a bad episode of *Survivor*.

Much to my mom's dismay, I'd grab empty canning jars from our basement (it wasn't *Little House on the Prairie*, but it was close), poke holes in the lids, and go out on a bug-finding safari all day long. I'd create mini-menageries in each jar, filling them with live butterflies, grasshoppers, beetles, ladybugs, dragonflies, and sowbugs. But my favorite?

Fireflies.

I'd wait excitedly until twilight, then my mom would spray me head-to-toe with extra-strength Off! (I felt like I was in the radiation decontamination scene with Meryl Streep from the movie *Silkwood* — "It Burns!") after which I'd set out under the twinkling and mosquito-infested night sky.

I soon became lost in a magical world where the entire backyard would flash on and off with flying incandescent lights of lightning-bug madness. They were *everywhere*.

But it wasn't enough for me to just watch. Or even capture the horny buggers. (I found out later that the flashing lights were used by cocky males to attract bored females. Sort of how my best friend in the 7th grade, Cathy Kincaid, would react to half our male student body as they tried to impress her with stupid, teenaged, machismo antics to no avail. Eye roll . . . talk to the hand . . . and . . . *dismissed*.)

Anyway, I wanted those fireflies to light up for me *personally*. (Sort of how I wished Cathy's suitors would ignore her skinny ass and just come flirt with me.) I wanted a Tony Light Show. So I would catch one with my hand, entombing it in my fist.

And herein, the conundrum. I wanted to see this little beetle create its pyrotechnics up close and personal. I had it in my hand, but in order to see the light (pun intended), I had to let go. Rats!

Let go.

So I did. And when I hadn't accidentally squashed the poor buggers — their taillights slowly flickering on and off before they'd permanently go dark (*Sorry!*) — I got to see what I'd wished for.

Bioluminescence.

The moral of the story: Stop squashing bugs! Or . . . Everything we want in life is waiting to reveal itself to us as soon as we let go.

Our culture has an obsession with control. We often think that if we let go, nothing will happen for us. But letting go is not an act of passivity. It doesn't mean that we give up, or stop, or throw in the towel. It means that we let go of our *resistance* and we surrender our desire to control. We learn to breathe into what *is*. Once we relinquish the need to control the outcome of a situation, we can step into the truth of the moment and what it wants to show us. We become available to what truly exists in that time and space, rather than what our controlling left brain *thinks* should be there.

Let go and let the moment show you.

You'll be surprised to see that there are figurative fireflies lighting up all around you. And perhaps a boyfriend or girlfriend (or two), waiting to demonstrate their own bioluminescent light show just for you.

M

MEET your edge.
It's something to face.
Then you'll discover life isn't a race.

L ife isn't a destination. There's nowhere to get to. *Oh, yes, there is, Tony. I want to go to New York and Paris and Rome.*

Okay, Woody Allen!

Once we get married (*sigh*), or book our TV show (*yee-haw!*), or win our award (*You like me . . . Right now . . . You like me!*), or buy our house (in a *Real Housewives* neighborhood, please), or any of the number of things we desire as the end goal, we'll discover that once we have them, our life is still the same.

Sort of.

Land a man. Marry a man. Divorce a man. Find a new man.

Book a job. Finish a job. Need a new job . . . Freak out! Shake, stir, and repeat.

Sure, the external, material trappings have changed (we've got more money, are finally famous, have the nice car, moved to a better zip code), but the core essence of who we are is carried with us. We think once we get to the culmination of the things we've been working hard to achieve that life will blow magical fairy dust on us and all will be resolved. Now I obviously like fairies, but they're not going to solve the problems that will still present themselves as we achieve our goals. Life's not designed that way. Nor should it be.

What *does* transform us is coming up against our "edge" (as inspirational Buddhist monk Pema Chödrön calls it), meeting it, and pushing through.[20] The pushing through to the other side of what scares us, or what makes us want to recoil, or what we have judgments about, is really what forges a new you.

And life is a constant calling towards the edge. It never ends. Ever. We may star in a movie, we may finally get that promotion, we may get our book published, or get engaged, but life will continue to confront us with our edge. This is because it's a path, a process, an unfolding journey — not a finish line.

Reaching new levels of anything simply asks us to overcome the new challenges that present themselves to us at a different vantage point. It's all relative. We've been waiting to get that huge promotion. But then once we do, we have a panic attack (*Where's my inhaler?*) because we doubt that we can even do the job.

We've been auditioning for acting jobs for the past three years to no avail and then suddenly book the lead in a new, network TV show. We pee our pants out of excitement and then collapse with paranoia thinking that they've hired the wrong person, or we're surely going to get fired, or we're going to stutter or forget all our lines, or embarrass ourselves.

We've been studying feverishly for over a year and are finally ready to take the bar exam. We fail. We immediately wonder if joining the traveling circus and becoming an operator of the Tilt-a-Whirl is a better career choice.

Life will force us to meet our edge. Over and over. It's not designed to break us. To make us give up. To stop us. It actually helps to smooth out our edges. It reveals to us areas of our life that need attention. Maybe it's cultivating patience. Or acceptance. Maybe it's about being more resolute or taking things less personally. Sometimes it's about forgiveness or letting go. There's always a deeper learning. If we remain open, it will reveal itself to us.

And these edges are important. Early in life they're sharp and pointy. They inflict wounds. On us and others. We ignore them or run away from them and they continue to damage and cause pain because of our avoidance. But as we begin to simply acknowledge them, they have this amazing ability to transform us.

Like sharp, craggy rocks that have been unearthed from a cliff and deposited by rockslides from their mountain perch, they lie sharp and jagged on the shore. *Ouch.* Stepping on them hurts. So we try to go the other way. But there's only one path.

Never around, always through.

Eventually (*gulp!*), we walk the walk. The earth's weathering elements do their work on them and on us. Wind and biting rain, ice and the ocean's waves begin to erode the rocks. They're battered and chiseled, chaffed and scuffed (sort of how it feels to be tossed about by our life's challenges) until they end up these beautifully soft, polished, shiny stones.

Our edges have been polished by our life challenges and experiences. By allowing that natural process to occur — because it must and *will* happen — we discover that weathering subsequent storms gets easier and easier. More tolerable. Less dramatic. And ultimately more rewarding.

Because getting the "stuff" is great. But getting our stuff and having pushed through our edge to get there is even greater.

Sort of how a diamond must feel after it emerges from its thick, brittle casing of coal.

Diamonds, like us, are made in the rough. Still more edges to overcome, but shining ever so brightly, because of them.

N

NEUROPLASTICITY.

A scientific term
to get our brains to affirm and confirm.

As a 20-something living in the constantly stimulating city of New York, I often felt my brain corresponded to the pulse of the city. You know; throbbing, noisy, loud, unruly, neurotic, and sometimes dirty.

At the time, I didn't think that there might be an alternative to city life. "Of course there is Tony . . . The Hamptons!" But I was thinking more like peace, gentleness, repose, solitude, calmness. "You mean we can feel these things while still living *in* the city?" Yep.

I didn't have access to those states of mind because I often acted out of my reptilian brain. That's right, there was a part of me (and each of us) that's just a little Komodo dragon. (And if you've ever seen those lizards munching on a decomposing carcass, it just ain't pretty. Gross.)

That reptilian part of our brain is the oldest part of our evolving brain and is primarily concerned with reptilian things: survival, hoarding, dominance. Emotionally and behaviorally, these characteristics can show up in our lives in the form of resistance, fear, and defensiveness.

At the age of 23, I didn't know I was acting like a lizard. I often reacted to situations from this reptilian fight-or-flight response. As reptiles should. Having no other skills to rely upon, the first response triggered in my brain (generally fear-related) is what I'd go with.

Scream. *That sounds good.* Cry (Crocodile Tears). *Go for it.* Gnash my teeth and pummel my chest. *Yes.* Say something nasty and run in the other direction. *Awesome.*

That may work for an Iguana — that's why they've been around for millions of years — but it doesn't work for human beings. Well, it kind of does in the short term; but in the long term, scarcity thinking, taking things personally, being a victim, and rationalizing the hell out of something never serve us. The wonderful thing, however, is that we have a higher brain, too, that gives us access to the potential of who we can become. We can replace salamander sarcasm with optimism, crocodilian complaining with gratitude, amphibian anxiety with acceptance. (Sorry, I couldn't resist those monitor lizard metaphors.)

Neuroplasticity is all about rebuilding and restructuring the architecture of our brains by creating new neural grooves to replace old ones that have been created by sheer repetitive use. It's like trying to work with new software on a Mac but our operating system is still set up for a PC.

This requires us to rewire our brains. It sounds easy. And in many ways, it is.

By the time I was in my late 20s I realized that constantly acting out of my neuroses wasn't helping me. A friend invited me to a meditation. "What the hell is that?" I thought. Intrigued to hear some Indian swami speak, I strapped on my silver-tipped rollerblades (as one did in the '90s); wore my blue, one-piece, lycra roller-blading outfit (it was sort of like the onesies Mormons wear, except rather than being made out of scratchy polyester, my onesie was sheer and shiny and *fabulous!*); turned on my favorite Walkman cassette (singing to the tunes of Salt-n-Pepa and Bell Biv DeVoe); and skated my way to Shangri-La.

When I got there (fashionably late) I was greeted by a hushed silence of 200 people sitting in absolute stillness. Ummmm . . . what were these people doing? I tiptoed toward my friend only to be accosted by two ushers who I assumed were extending me a personal welcome. *Namaste* to you, too! They showered me with lots of silk scarves. ("Oh, how exotic," I thought. "People from India are *so* nice. Free gifts!") And then they proceeded to wrap me in them. Pigs-in-a-blanket-style.

Apparently, it was disrespectful to show as much skin (*scandal!*) as my lycra number revealed (I did sort of look like I was auditioning for Cirque de Soleil's popular X-rated show). By the time I sat down next to my friend (who did a double-take at my new get-up), I was an indigo, marigold, and sepia-hued, Saran-wrapped mummy from head to roller-bladed toe, looking part belly dancer, part Bollywood star, part *Ali Baba and the Forty Thieves*. Or Sally Field (yes, her again) trying to rescue her daughter dressed in a quasi-Burka in that '80s tearjerker, *Not without My Daughter*!

As I sat — in my layers of *I Dream of Jeannie*-wear — listening to the yogi talking about "grace", I was suddenly transported to an ocean of silence.

That was the beginning. I realized that there were possibilities for the brain to experience states beyond its endless, incessant, unpleasant chatter. Just because I said things to myself didn't make them true. Negative phrases and beliefs I repeated to myself didn't make them factual. The things going on in our heads don't make us sane. In fact, it's usually the opposite.

Many scientists and doctors now suggest that the brain is but a part of a bigger dimension known as the mind, or consciousness, that can lead us to whole new insights about ourselves, possibility, and creativity.

UCLA research scientist Dr. Valerie Hunt says, "I think we have way overrated the brain as the active ingredient in the relationship of a human to the world. It's just a really good computer. But the aspects of the mind that have to do with creativity, imagination, spirituality, and all those things, I don't see them in the brain at all. The mind's not in the brain. It's in that darn [quantum] field."[21]

Doctor and spiritualist Deepak Chopra says, "Thoughts are probability waves from the conditioned mind that shape everyday reality. True creativity comes from pure consciousness."[22]

So by developing new neurons in our brain to change the repetitive patterns of our thoughts, we can shape our lives differently. Our reality — which is created from possibility waves converting into particles (matter) through thought — can be altered as we become more mindful of what we're thinking. And as we begin to experience a part of ourselves that *isn't* our thoughts, we tap into consciousness. Something beyond ourselves. A *gap between thoughts*, if you will, that is more like wide-open spaces where we'll discover the neural noise in our heads can become quieter, less assaultive, less stressful. It doesn't always have to sound like the intersection at 42nd Street and Broadway at rush hour.

Or even if it does, we'll have access to other neural roads, too. Like ones that will take us to the Central Park of our minds. Green. Fertile. Relaxing. Rejuvenating. So we can be in the action of the city, but still far removed from it at the same time. Isn't that, after all, the best of both worlds?

O

OCCAM's Razor.
A nifty phrase.
Don't jump to silly conclusions
when the truth might simply amaze.

I sit typing this chapter while downing a glass—errr . . . a *bottle* of wine. It seems I've been stood up on a date. I know. I know. You're probably thinking, "Who could stand you up, Tony?" *Well, that's what I said!* But I'm also thinking a number of things, like, "Who says, 'Sorry I can't meet up . . . I have no wheels . . . my car's pistons broke'?"

Take the bus!

Other negative neural grooves get triggered: "Maybe I'm too old." Or, "I guess I'm not attractive enough." Or, "I guess he's just not that into me." (And to prove it, they made a movie about it starring Drew Barrymore.)

I think I need another drink.

Somewhere between my second and third (bottle), I have an epiphany. I'm reminded of the law of simplicity. Which sadly, no one taught Drew in the movie, so she, too, became a victim of dating lots of losers who left bad "broken pistons" excuses on her voicemail.

Occam's Razor.

The simplest explanation for something is generally the *correct* explanation for something that may *seem* to have many hypotheses. The answer that has the least amount of assumptions is usually the truth.

So maybe my dream date really did blow his pistons. Why should I think otherwise? Because we humans like to *assume*. And then make lots of assumptions on top of those assumptions. And before we know it, we're spinning worst-case scenarios and doom-and-gloom stories about our lives.

You know the ones. The agent didn't sign you. The only probable answer . . . you suck. You didn't get the callback. *Duh*. You're talentless. You don't pass the job interview. Pretty obvious. You failed.

Or . . .

The agent didn't sign you because you reminded him of his ex-girlfriend . . . who he's now suing. You didn't get the callback because they already made an offer to someone else . . . like Channing Tatum. The job interview? They consolidated the job into a new position and it's being handled . . . by a robot . . . in *China!*

Human nature likes to *react*. That's how we get to the buzzer first on *Family Feud* and win lots of prizes. But our reacting to things without clarity and objectivity hurts. When science says we have around 60,000 to 70,000 thoughts a day and 95% of them are thoughts we habitually think ("I suck!") and 80% of those are *negative* ("I *really, really* suck!"), that indicates that we operate on autopilot for most of our lives.

Especially when something emotional occurs and triggers our neural noise response system and we let the habit kick in. Next time this happens, stop, drop, and roll. Well, not exactly. That might look a little odd as you stand in line at the Starbucks. (Although it might get you a free triple-pump mocha.) But yes. *Stop* the thought. *Drop* the habit. And then *roll* with a more neutral and simple explanation for the event that occurred.

In time, you'll begin to see that the simplest explanation *was* the explanation. And generally, the truth.

Another way of thinking about it is *K.I.S.S.* No, not the rock group that was overshadowed by Gene Simmons's flexible tongue.

Keep. It. Simple. Silly.

With simplicity and patience, things (and people) eventually reveal their true nature. Or — thanks to the wonders of modern technology, like Facebook stalking — you can always speed up the process.

Voilà! In just a few hours, I found out the simplest answer to the reason I got stood up. Apparently my piston-poisoned amore's car *is* getting lots of tune-ups these days . . . by his *boyfriend!!* Hmmm . . . I don't remember hearing him say he had one when we planned our date.

So, even if it's not always the answer we want to hear, staying steadfast in simplicity cuts through the confusion and chaos our minds like to create.

What you need to remember is to give yourself a *KISS*.

Especially when it seems no one else wants to.

P

PURPOSE.

It's what we're all here for.
And it holds a key to unlocking our door
to joy and success and a whole lot more.

The purpose-driven life. (Do you have one? If you don't . . . are you freaking out?) That phrase almost feels as if we have to find "it". *Purpose.* That it's hidden from us (Under a rock? Behind a tree?) and it requires us to *do* something in order for our lives to have meaning. If we don't, we're screwed.

You don't have to go looking for it. "Is it here? Is it in Africa? Is it being an artist? Is it working with children? Can I only know it if I find Jesus or Buddha or become a vegetarian or digitally upload my life onto Facebook for the entire world to see? Should I be doing something else? Oh, shit! I'm lost!"

Your life already *has* purpose. By simply *being.*

Someone's life isn't more purposeful because he or she reaches millions of people via a YouTube video that goes viral, compared to a homeless man on the street. Purpose equals value. And every life — all life — is purposeful because of the connective tapestry that it weaves. There is intrinsic value in *all* things. And it's not because of the external labeling we overlay onto people and things.

So purpose isn't created in what we do (which is a very Westernized, ego-centered way of thinking that measures purpose through achievement), or how we're defined, or what we *think* about ourselves, but instead dwells within who we *are.*

Our presence is our purpose. How we *show up* in our lives, whoever we are, is purpose. It's created by being more present with what's in front of us right now. Living more totally. More fully. It's not about being a multi-tasking whiz: talking to someone while checking our Google calendar, responding to texts, sending emails, tweeting, watching an episode of *Downton Abbey* (all on our phone!), and worrying about what's going to happen in the future. It's not about placing ego demands on ourselves that we have to change the world, or become famous, or make millions of dollars, or live in Bel Air, or do it for our parents, or not let anyone down, or "make good with our life." It's not about our lives having greater meaning if we do something philanthropic or charitable.

True purpose transcends career ego-labeling or how we define ourselves. Purpose is created in the details of the moment. And those change from moment to moment. So therefore, our purpose does, too. It's not a fixed thing. Or a destination. It's fluid and changeable.

So yes, purpose can be realized by being more charitable, or performing a job you love, or raising a family. But it can also occur in so many other ways. Like smiling at a stranger. Or slowing down. Or listening instead of talking. It can occur by being engaged totally and serving your work completely — whether you're a factory worker or farmer. It can occur by being grateful, and loving what we do, and taking pride in what we contribute. Expanding what it is that we already do to serve others. It can be accomplished by being more mindful of sustainability, lessening our footprint, doing things with greater intention and awareness. Turning off the lights. Riding a bike instead of driving our cars. Consuming less, creating more. Mindfully breathing. Sitting in silence. Thinking before we speak. Planting a tree. Surrendering more.

We're constantly missing the call of purpose because we're so distracted by our ego needs ("How do I look?" "Will this sell?" "Am I popular?" "What will they think of me?" "How do I sound?").

Real purpose is about discovering, finally and completely, that we are enough.

Period.

Who we are is perfection.

Look at a newborn baby. Do we see anything in a baby's face but love? Anything in a baby's eyes but innocence? Anything in this creation but potential? We come from that. We still *are* that. But for some reason we don't believe it. So we work hard — *really hard* — to be clever or funny or hot or sexy or charming, thinking *that's* how we'll find our purpose.

We apologize for our existence; for taking up too much space, or not trusting we have something to contribute. We feel badly for speaking our minds, or taking a stand, or being different, or asking the waiter to refill our water glass. We assume roles to compensate for our perceived lack. We laugh extra loud, we pontificate, we try to be provocative, we become "experts", we attempt to stand out in the crowd.

You already are a standout because you're *you*.

There's something you're capable of doing that is inherently unique and different than anyone else's way of doing that same thing. That is derived by the way you express yourself through that thing.

Purpose suggests we have to be recognized, awarded, or applauded for our work. We don't. Indeed, for most of us on this planet, we never will be. But that doesn't make us less worthy or less fantastic.

Engage with the world as if it were your Olympic Stadium or Broadway stage or self-named theme park. Not because we seek attention. But because those environments — which happen to (usually) bring out the best of the triumphant *spirit* and *passion* and *creativity* in each person — represent what is already inside each of us, regardless of whether or not we ever get on *The Voice* or qualify for the Olympic medal round in Tae Kwon Do.

I often joke to many actors with whom I work: "Save it for the stage!"

But I've got it all wrong. *Don't* save it for the stage. Or anywhere else. Stop believing your essence and what you have to share is a limited resource that is non-renewable and has to be preserved. For whom? For what?

The more you engage, the more you'll have to give away. And the more you give away, the more you'll develop a deeper and more present *you*. But you must start with yourself. If you start anywhere else, it's been said, it's a false start and you'll just be forced to go back to the starting line and begin again. And again.

You have limitless reserves of innate *potential*. Sociologist Abraham Maslow comments on this when he says, "Musicians must make music, artists must paint, poets must write if they are to be ultimately at peace with themselves. What human beings can be, they must be. They must be true to their own nature. This need we may call self-actualization . . . It refers to man's desire for self-fulfillment, namely to the tendency for him to become *actually* in what he is *potentially*: to become everything that one is capable of becoming."[23]

Now *that's* purpose.

Q

QUITTER.
That's not the true spirit of man.
The person who achieves is the one who thinks he can.

In the 5th grade, I quit baseball. I hated it. I prayed the ball would never fly to me in the far-right outfield (but of course it would) and I'd cringe behind my over-sized mitt attempting lamely to coerce it into the "sweet spot" (whatever the hell that was) only to have it crash on my head.

It knocked me out. I awakened to a bruised temple and incredulous stares. No one cared. (These were the days when kids mostly went unsupervised. We survived. When something bad happened it was usually greeted with a collective "Ugh!" Then we'd pick up and continue where we left off, barring any broken limbs or bloody noses.)

I, on the other hand, had had enough. I dramatically threw my glove at my coach, jumped on my green, banana-seat, Schwinn bicycle, and pedaled home as fast as I could. My mom found me sobbing in my basement and I begged her to let me do *anything* else — like bake cakes or organize the Parks & Recreation talent competition — just no more baseball. She agreed. Thank *Gawd*.

I quit because I was scared. I had two older brothers who were, like, state league champions or something and my parents *naturally* assumed I'd know how to play. I showed no skill or talent nor even any joy in playing, but that's what parents did with their kids back in the day. Throw them in.

Had I loved the sport but was scared, quitting wouldn't have been an option. So let's be clear on that first. Quit . . . by all means . . . quit (!) things you feel you have no passion for. Yes. You heard me say it. Your true skills are waiting to be expressed somewhere else, so if you're not in it, quit it.

But the tricky thing about the anatomy of baseball — or any endeavor — is that had I been properly taught how it all works, the understanding I would have gained would have minimized my fears and I probably would have grown to like it. And maybe even become a league champion.

We'll never know. Things take time. And when fear is our first reaction to something, it clouds our vision. It prevents us from having any kind of insight. And we quit.

The *gap* between my panic-inducing fear of baseball and the actual joy of playing was too wide to be traversed. And life is about *shortening* the divide between where we are and where we'd like to be. But most of us bail when the distance seems too large, or insurmountable, or worse: You don't even realize you're in the gap. And I don't mean the store.

Think about it. You want to get healthier or lose weight. You want to have a more committed spiritual practice. You want to be more creative and generate more creative work. The only way you're going to get there is to keep going. There's no other solution. No quick fix. And that's how you shorten the gap.

The host of NPR's "This American Life", Ira Glass, talks about shortening the gap in the creative process between our creative desires and our output of work. He says that when we first begin to create, we do so because we have "great taste."[24] (Hah! Little does he know, I started creating because I wanted 7th grade hottie Philip Mancuso to notice me.) But as we start creating, our work is bad. (*Well, duh.* If only I could take back that poem I wrote to Philip about love being "fleeting; like geese flying south for the winter.") Our creations don't fulfill the picture we have in our minds of what we want to be doing. (*Philip, I was a neophyte.*)

Most people stop during this phase. Mr. Glass says there's only one way to get to where we want to go in our creative lives: Don't quit.

By continuing to do the work, you eventually start to create better and better work. Work you're excited about. Work that means something. Work you can be proud of.

"Dear Philip. Love is fleeting. Dodging and weaving, ever deceiving." (*Take that, you stupid geese rhyme.*)

I think the biggest gap we need to shorten is the divide we create by judging our creative selves. We say such unkind things to ourselves that we shut down creativity before a creative impulse has truly had a chance to take root and flower.

The judgments force stoppage.

The only way we're going to get past the loudness of the noise in our heads is by doing. Constantly. And eventually, the outpouring of work exceeds the things we say about ourselves. That's the tipping point. And we've then shortened the gap and gotten to the other side.

We'll still want to quit. For sure. That's normal. We'll still come up with every excuse in the baseball handbook to get out of doing the work. We'll procrastinate. We'll convince ourselves we're doing something else productive (like watching *What Would Ryan Lochte Do?* – "Jeah!"), knowing very well we aren't.

If we can't get out of it, then we'll eventually go to bat — whether that's a dance class, or facing a blank computer screen to begin writing, or going to an audition — and we'll strike out. Or, we'll bunt. We'll draw a foul. We'll make it to second but abort making it to third. We'll drop the ball. We'll allow way too many runs, we'll load the bases, we'll be replaced in the 7th inning, and lots of times our ass will simply sit on the bench.

But every now and again — the more we stay in the game and discover that the gap isn't insurmountable after all — we'll actually hit a home run.

And *that's* the sweet spot.

R

RECOGNITION & RECOVERY.

That can only happen when you make the discovery.

A lot of what life (and this book) is about is realizing how we get stuck, sabotage ourselves, get in our own way, or make questionable choices in life. We all do. That Ogilvie home perm I tried in the '80s, Carrot Top deciding to go all Iron Man a few years ago and move to Las Vegas and wear really tight tank tops, or anyone attempting to pull off culottes (aka capris pants)! These "mistakes" are part of what make us who we are. The goal is to not repeat them.

Ignorance is bliss, they say. But if you remain ignorant forever, it's just . . . well . . . ignorance. Ignorance of your true nature. Of what's possible for you. Of what's holding you back.

In my 20s I was so neurotic and stuck in my head (surprise), I didn't even know what "recognizing" where I was stuck was. Nowadays, my life is about recognizing when I do things that keep me out of the flow.

I react and stop breathing. I use limited left-brain thinking to give meaning to situations that haven't fully developed. I beat myself up, shove my feelings down, tune out, and complain. I assume. I bitch. I distract myself with Snapchat. I overeat, or smoke, or catastrophe-ize, or blame. I throw pity parties for one where I drink, plot revenge, whine (and drink more wine!), throw tantrums, judge, compare and despair, and freak out.

Sound familiar?

These choices don't give me access to deeper, more meaningful, and better-feeling choices. They are closed systems. They are designed to close me down and shut others out. They actually shut me out from *me*, where the only major significant insight is going to occur. But recognizing when those habits kick into gear is also the key to being released from them.

And that's simply Recognition and Recovery.

Recognize where you are. And recover quickly from anything that doesn't support you and make you feel good right now. Ask yourself: Would I swallow poison? Would I step in front of a moving train? Would I eat moo goo gai pan that's possibly gone south? Probably not. (Unless you're obsessed with *Jackass* and want to audition for that show.) But for most of us, we recognize when we do things that are a bit dangerous (I was going to say stupid, but I don't want you to feel judged.) and we recover from our moments of temporary disconnect from reality.

Our society is so health conscious. We go to the gym. We drink protein shakes. We eat lots of acai berries. We switch to almond milk. So, why do we allow ourselves to ingest cerebral poison? Why do we cultivate consciousness that supports our feeling scared or alienated or less than?

By now (I mean we are at the letter "R"), we're probably aware that when we hear ourselves say toxic things, only *we* have the power to change them. And it is poison. Thinking of ourselves in terms of limitation, defeat, negativity, and depression *never* serves us. *Ever.* That's why it doesn't feel good. But we're often addicted to our bad-feeling thoughts because we've been thinking them for so long we don't know that alternative ways to think exist.

This is the recognition step. When we ingest something nuclear, spit it out. *It's nuclear!* Don't let it spread throughout our system poisoning us with doubt and despair and unhappiness.

The recovery step then occurs by replacing it with *anything* that feels better and is more accurate. Habits can be broken. They are just beliefs that have been thought continuously over time and have formed that reptilian groove of neural noise. As we know, we can create new grooves that don't sabotage us. So chuck out that sneaky snake by simply activating these two tools.

Recognition.

Recovery.

And when we do, we'll find that every day gets just a little bit easier to get out of our own way.

S

STAR!

How to become one when you already are.
(Especially in your living room
or when you're drunk at a bar!)

Y ou're a star. We all are.

Okay, I don't want to prolong your delusion into thinking you're somebody you're not. I don't want you rattling around in your Hollywood Hills bungalow surrounded by *lots* of cats and channeling a modern-day Norma Desmond from *Sunset Boulevard* ("All right, Mr. DeMille. I'm ready for my close-up.").

I mean *cosmically*, you're a star. Well, that may seem a little "woo-woo", too. A little Shirley MacLaine, *Out on a Limb*, beam-me-up-Scotty.

Let's start here.

Everything of mass in this physical reality is made of energy (see $E = mc^2$). As energetic beings, we are pure, positive, magnetic, creative, attraction-based energy. Our birthright is love. Our DNA is joy and intelligence. Staying aligned with this energy is the currency that moves us in the direction of the things that we desire in the world. And when we have a desire, it is birthed from that same energy that we already are. And that is star energy.

Think about it. When you have desires for things, what launches the desires in the first place are feelings of love, excitement, passion, joy, creativity, possibility, wonder. In short, you. Your essence. But you sidetrack yourself and cancel out your intentional desires because you get caught up in the left-brain dialogue that makes you feel like crap.

Then Senate candidate (Now Senator. Yay!) Elizabeth Warren gave an inspiring speech at the 2012 Democratic National Convention that, in part, responded to Mitt Romney's statement that "corporations are people."

"No, Governor Romney, corporations are *not* people. People have hearts. They have kids. They get jobs. They get sick. They cry. They dance. They live. They love. And they die. And that matters. That matters . . . because we do not run this country for corporations. We run it for people."[25]

Amen.

You are not analytics, algorithms, search engine optimization results. You are not a statistic, a price point, a demographic, a sale, a number of hits, a rating, a label. You are not your IMDb ranking, the number of tweet mentions you get, the Facebook friends you acquire, the happy faces or thumbs up you generate.

We can't let our cultural corporate model of comparing and then determining what's "hot" or "popular" or "in" squash the spirit of who we are. The spirit of who we are is limitless. There's science to prove it. We are made of the same stuff that stars are made.

Billions of years ago, before there were planets or the sun (or Tom Cruise), there was just space. Infinite space filled with subatomic particles that became atoms of hydrogen, which, through nuclear fusion, formed stars. Certain stars would blow up in dazzling supernovas, spewing matter from within their core over billions of miles. This matter, through gravitational pull, coalesced and later formed planets — including earth — and everything on the planets. Including you and I. (And Tom Cruise!)

So we *do* come from the heart of a star.

Catch yourself the next time you start corporatizing yourself. Put it into context; this trend or that fad, this popularity contest or that "it" thing will pass in a blip of time. (Sort of like those T-Rexes and Brontosauruses — actually, they're called Apatosauruses now — that the Kentucky Creation Museum says were passengers on Noah's Ark.)

Really? (How did Noah keep himself from getting eaten, I wonder?)

But what we are is infinite. We are the heart of a star.

T

TIME.

It makes the world go 'round.
But what if it were actually something that simply can't be found?

Tricky. This thing called "time".

We rely on it. We keep track of it. We try to speed it up; slow it down. Try to reverse it. We look in the mirror (*gasp!*) and see the ravages of it. (Unless those Botox injections have permanently frozen your face into looking like a smooth baby's butt!)

We race against it. We curse it. We waste it.

But what if "it" wasn't real? At all.

Since the dawn of humanity, mankind has relied on varying signs and symbols in nature, the planets, and the seasons in order to carve out tangible constructs of time. Paleolithic hunter-gatherers' relationship to time was created through their experience with the cosmos; through patterns of planetary, solar, and lunar movements. Time, to them, was cyclical, as it is in nature. The planets are orbs, the sun is a circle of yellow heat, the seasons loop from one phase to the next, only to come full circle and repeat again and again.

There was no separation between man and nature. It was experienced as integration, as a whole, with their relationships always set in the present. Everything leading back to itself.

As evolution continued and morphed into the Neolithic period, time — and homosapiens' relationship to it — forever changed. With domestication and the advent of agriculture, humans engaged with the world in a new way. This material involvement with the environment caused what physicist Adam Frank calls "The Big Bang of Consciousness", and is the "root cause of all the innovations and revolutions that followed."[26]

Basically, cities emerged and political and religious systems were put in place in order to dominate and control its citizens. The concept of time became a tool to support those governing bodies. Calendars were created to celebrate religious holidays, which in turn promoted religious ideology, and "The Church" became the de facto government, dictating and controlling time.

The industrial revolution then gave birth to a new understanding of time: that it equals money. This forever altered our relationship to time and work.

Hello, 9-to-5.

As time and our understanding of it evolved (de-volved?), mankind's personal experiences in relating to the world also changed. We no longer saw ourselves as a harmonious part of the whole. We saw ourselves existing as separate entities designed to dominate and control the whole.

Our conscious relationship to self became linear. We became mentally disconnected from the guidance of the wholeness and connectivity that a circle brings. In Hindu mythology and Buddhism, the wheel of life — the circle — is at the forefront of existence. It actually *is* existence itself. Instead of time being linear, it's a never-ending circle, a folding and unfolding loop of growth: creation, preservation, destruction. Brahma. Vishnu. Shiva. Birth, death, re-birth.

Meanwhile, our bodies themselves are aligned with circles: circadian rhythms for sleep patterns, women's menstruation cycles, the replenishing of cells every seven to ten years. But we like to view our lives according to timelines. We look at things from the perspective of where we *were* and where we're *going*, and often disconnect from what's happening right now. We see our lives as a continuum punctuated by benchmarks — life "events" — that are almost always based in the future. You know the ones. Turning 18, going to college, our first love, our first real adult job, our first vacation, our first apartment, our first and hopefully only (unless you're like Susan Lucci's character on *All My Children*) engagement and marriage. Our collective mantra is, "I can't wait until . . ."

Ironically, most of our lives are spent *between* these "events", these moments of trying to get somewhere. In our fixation on our future timeline, we constantly miss now.

Well, let's understand what "now" means in relation to transcending "time".

There is scientific research that supports that time is a lot more fluid than we think, and it actually has more to do with the illusion of motion than it does with being a fixed entity. Time is not absolute. In the quantum world, particles — scientists have discovered — can move backwards. If subatomic particles can interact across all space and time, might it be that larger matter (ummmm . . . the universe?) exists in some vast here and now where all points in space and time are experienced in a single instant?

Physicist Robert Lanza thinks so.

"Instead of time having an absolute reality, imagine instead that existence is like a sound recording. . . . Depending on where the needle is placed, you hear a certain piece of music. This is what we call the present. The music, before and after the song now being heard, is what we call the past and the future. Imagine, in like manner, every moment and day enduring in nature always. The record does not go away. All nows (all the songs on the vinyl record) exist simultaneously, although we can only experience the world (or the record) piece by piece."[27]

In the context of aging and life span, we can see another example of how time is not absolute, nor sequential. As children, we don't have imprinted memory in our existence because life is so new; like a memory card that's not full. But, as we develop and move on with our lives, "things become compressed," says Frank.[28] We have so much memory built up on our cards and we also recognize that we're getting older. So, as our memory cards get full, we begin to contextualize our life in terms of how much we've lived and how much we have left, and the illusion of it is that time is moving faster. But as Einstein said, "The distinction between past, present, and future is only a stubbornly persistent illusion."[29]

Some people say our most precious gift is to give people our time. But how can that be if it's an illusion?

Instead, start giving people something real. Give them your presence. Be with them *totally*. Share significantly. Stop withholding.

What if we started living our lives like the ancient Australian Aborigines? They had no contextual understanding of time. Instead, they lived in what they called the ever-present "Everywhen".[30]

Always here. Always now. Everything always happening simultaneously at once. No past. No future. No beginning. No end. Just this perpetual experience of now.

Isn't that the experience we're all after anyway? Moments of timelessness, deep connection, and love that sit within this very brief construct of time that we've each been given and each manage in our own way every day?

We're all reaching for experiences of transcendence that lie outside "time", mistakenly thinking that time is what generates these moments to begin with. It doesn't. And maybe that's why, no matter what we try, time cannot be grasped. That's because it's impossible to hold on to something that's not real.

So instead of fretting over something that *seems* real but is actually illusory, what if we got present to what *seems* illusory but is actually the only thing that is real?

Now.

U

UNKNOWN.

What we often run away from.
But inside this matrix, all creative things come.

*E*verything we want is in the Unknown.

You're probably thinking, "Ummm . . . I *know* where I can get a pair of Jimmy Choos for half off, so actually that's not quite true."

What I'm talking about is the physics of creativity, not the end result of beating down our fellow shoppers to get our hands on that last Ashley Olsen mini at Mervyn's.

We listen to the pseudo-self (our ego), which tells us that the Unknown is a scary and unsafe place to be simply because it's unfamiliar. (Well it is! Haven't you seen *The Texas Chainsaw Massacre*?) So the ego will do everything it can to prevent us from going there. Even though going there is where we need to go. (Except for going in *that barn* in *The Texas Chainsaw Massacre*!)

But a deeper part of us craves the Unknown; desires it. The adventurer — the seeker in us — knows that all expansion in life, all discoveries, all creative victories have only occurred by stepping into that which is unfamiliar.

Look at our own lives. Anything that we've accomplished that has been meaningful or significant or fulfilling has required that we *first* step into that which is foreign. Sometimes, that's *literally* foreign. A trip to Zimbabwe, anyone? Sometimes it's figurative, like asking someone out on a date.

But we have to take the leap.

Because our minds tells us things like "You're going to get hurt." "Don't be stupid." "You can never do that." "You're crazy!" "Who are you to try that?" — and on and on — it feels almost counter-intuitive to step into the void.

The void generates all that noise and mind clutter in the first place. The "What ifs?"

But the Unknown is really just a scary word for something that is actually the creative matrix. Infinite potential. It's the molding clay, the blank canvas, the substance needed for our creative genius to take root and grow. The Unknown plugs us into universal consciousness — a stream of information and ideas we cannot access without first taking the leap.

I know it seems in our nature to have everything figured out first, but that's just the control mechanism that overrides our natural inclination to lean toward the adventure. Think about all the things that we felt sure of, for which we *knew* the answers. Didn't all of those things work out differently than we planned anyway?

So, what's the big deal? There's a part of us that's always going to be seeking things for which we never seem to actually have the answers. That's part of the mystery of being here on this planet. Sometimes "knowing" is the booby prize. *Waa-waa.*

We've heard the expression, "If I knew then what I know now, I'd never have done it." That statement right there is an example of how we'd stop experiencing things if we always knew *beforehand* what we were about to embark on. We'd stop taking the adventure. We'd stop trying. We'd give up. We'd concede defeat. Yes, a lot of times it doesn't work out the way we think it will, but that doesn't mean the experience wasn't worth the . . . well . . . experience.

All aspects of our journey are what make the journey.

So our "unknowingness" is essential for us to live and experience and grow. By having the experience, we gain knowledge. That's how we come to know.

As Einstein said, "Knowledge is experience. Anything else is information."[31] For knowledge to be gained from experience, it first requires us to step into the vast field of unknown possibility.

So jump in a little more fervently. Watch what happens in our life. We might end up abandoning those Jimmy Choos completely and start going barefoot for a while. In Zimbabwe. Or maybe, simply, our own backyard.

V

VICTORIES.
You want them. We all do.
Relaxation is the key to get you through.

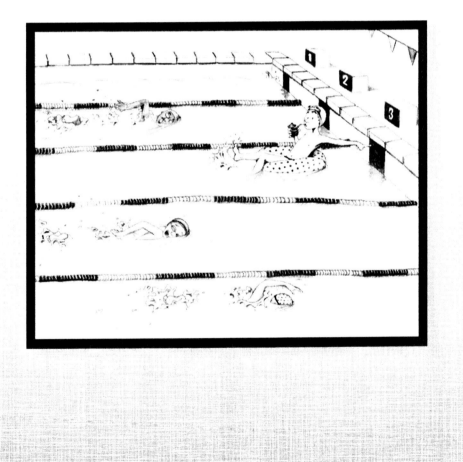

R elaxation.

It's always a breath away.

But we often forget this when we get stressed, tense our bodies, and attempt to go for something big. It almost seems counter-intuitive to relax when what we want seems to come from moments of committed self-exertion.

The 2012 London Olympics illustrated countless moments of achieving victories through relaxation. American swimmer Missy Franklin talked about her teammate Michael Phelps and how his key to getting through his program and winning events was . . . Relaxation. (And, ummmm, she obviously applied it herself as she ended up winning four gold medals!) U.S. Track & Field runner Sanya Richards, who won the 400 meters, was profiled in a *New York Times* article, illustrating how the key to her winning races was through . . . Relaxation. (See a theme here?)

In the story, sports physiologist Michael Joyner comments that runners who tense up during races "moved more slowly" making them "less efficient biomechanically [because the runner] expends the same amount of energy but doesn't travel as far." The article goes on to say that, "Some coaches and doctors, including Joyner, instruct runners to let their eyes droop during a race, hoping that if they relax their face, the rest of the body will follow." And it has proven to work.[32]

Relaxation.

There is an equivalent to this art (and science) of relaxation in everything we do. From playing tennis to illustrating graphics to singing opera to writing a play.

Jack Nicholson, when talking to actors, says that, "Eighty-five percent of you is exactly like the character you're playing, and isolating the other 15 percent and deciding how to act it is beginning the analysis. And the 85 percent that is you is the main element of all acting — which is relaxation so you are not overwhelmed by the tension and pressure of acting."[33]

But we are often unconscious of how we work against ourselves when we begin to strain and create resistance, both physically and mentally. In the creative process, the battles in the left brain generate fear, and our bodies take on the physical tension of that mental strain and neural noise.

For a performer or singer, it might manifest as clenching of the jaw, shutting feeling down, not releasing the voice, or narrowing the channel through which feeling can be released. For a runner, it can appear as physically getting tight, raising one's shoulders, and forgetting to inhale. For a businesswoman who wishes to make a career change, it could be experienced in the self-dialogues in her head that make her feel anxious or depressed and thereby shut down her ability to create.

The only way we can be free of that resistance is first, knowing that we are tightening up — mentally and physically — and second, relaxing so that we have access to all the other stuff that's getting squeezed out in the first place. Sometimes it's as simple as remembering to breathe. Sometimes it's expressing the mental noise outwardly, either through a vocal release (e.g., crying, laughing, letting go of a pure sound, screaming, or shouting) or getting physical.

Actually, all of these expressions are connected to breathing, so it's a reminder that everything truly is a breath away.

Forget, for a moment, about being at the Olympics or at The Met. Just in our daily lives, we often have little access to relaxation, not because it's not available to us, but because we think if we "relax" we're slacking off or shirking our responsibilities. Let's be clear on this concept. Relaxation does not mean sitting on the couch and catching up on all the episodes of our favorite reality shows we missed. It doesn't entail going to our local day spa and giving ourselves a mani-pedi with a complimentary mimosa. It's not firing up our bong and playing Xbox for 10 hours straight.

The kind of relaxation we're talking about here requires consciousness and awareness. It's not detaching from the world and our activities; it's staying in them and paying attention to the tension in our body and our breath while doing so.

As our boss yells at us, or we don't hear back from that girl we had a date with and really liked; as our car gets towed or we miss our connecting flight, we immediately feel stress. We compound the stress by doing the innumerable things we've been discussing in previous chapters that contribute to our left brain's incessant chatter. Our anxiety rises, we fast-forward, we catastrophe-ize. A vicious mental loop of conditioned thoughts gets triggered, which finds its own expression in our bodies (our fists clench shut, we feel anger and helplessness, our breathing gets shallow) and our brain releases endorphins that contribute to that mental and physical tension.

We simply check out. An automated stress system takes over and we get stuck. This is when mindfulness of relaxation can lead to daily mini-victories.

Life has a way of self-correcting itself. If we try to recall the things we totally flipped out about exactly a year ago today, we probably can't remember them. That's because they worked out! We make the speed bumps of our lives gigantic, molten-spewing volcanoes of drama and suffering. We don't need to. We can breathe. We can smile. We can remind ourselves that "this too shall pass." Because it will.

And even when things don't work out the way we want, ultimately — in the moment — we've all been equipped with the resources to overcome them. Resources of the Mind. Body. Spirit. They allow us to launch again. And again.

So the next time we feel ourselves getting tight and all our energy moving into our left brain, keeping us stuck in our head — do what Missy, Michael, Sanya, and all the rest of the Olympic champions do . . .

Breathe.

And we'll find that our victories are truly a relaxation away.

W

WAITING.
You really can't postpone.
Life is for the living,
as there's really no such thing as a loan.

Waiting is highly overrated. Especially for patience-challenged people like myself, or members of the in-famous 1970s circus act, The Flying Wallendas, whose family is a who's-who of thrill-seeking tightrope walkers. I think it was the patriarch of that high-walking clan who said, "Life is being on the wire. Everything else is just waiting."[34]

Well, easy for you to say, Karl. Most of us have a hard time just walking a straight line on a daily basis let alone one on a tiny wire strung 100 feet up in the air.

We wait for the better airfare, or for the date we went out with last week to call, or for permission. We wait until we lose 10 pounds, or until we get our haircut, or until we're "more prepared". We wait to get new headshots, or write that novel, or ask that person out. We end up spending so much time "waiting" for the right moment, that eventually the things we were "waiting" to do . . . slowly disappear from our lives. They become long-lost dreams that, for some reason, we seem to be okay with not having anymore.

Remember the dreams you used to have? Where have they gone? That operatic aria you wanted to sing? That trip to Bermuda you wanted to take? That idea for a drawing you wanted to sketch? They haven't gone any-where, you've just abandoned them.

So when is the right moment?

Now.

Stop waiting for something to get better or easier or less busy.

It won't.

Stop saying that you need to wait to be better organized, or more secure, or more sure of yourself.

You won't.

Stop waiting for the girlfriend, or the husband, or the agent, or the manager.

They don't.

Stop waiting for someone or some *thing* to give you permission to be all that you already are.

They can't.

Stop waiting for the right look, or the right age, or the right time, or the right resume.

You can't.

Stop putting your life on hold thinking you're still missing something in order for you to do the things you want to be doing.

You can do them all now.

Everything on this planet is going to expire. You will. Your friends. Your family. Your pet. Things you possess. Your favorite t-shirt. Things in your immediate environment. That tree in your backyard. Even the planet. Everything has a shelf life.

We buy things and let them expire because we keep waiting for the perfect time to partake of them. We're waiting for the perfect event. The magical moment.

The magic is alive here and now.

I looked through my refrigerator the other day to see what items had long since expired. I found some chocolate pudding from 2003. Was I waiting to make chocolate soufflé for some magical boyfriend who never appeared? I could have been enjoying my own delicious chocolate pudding. Screw the imaginary boyfriend!

Why do we wait to open that vintage bottle of wine? Sure it may taste better with that perfect person. But we'll be waiting a very long time because *perfection* doesn't exist. Drink it. Down it. Chug it. Forget the glass. Just enjoy it. Make the wonderful bouillabaisse with it that you've always wanted to try but (surprise!) *waited* for that romantic dinner for the past five years to test it out.

Stop postponing. Stop procrastinating. Stop letting things run past their expiration dates.

Look through your pantry. For each thing you find in your kitchen or in your fridge whose expiration date has long passed, do one thing that you've been postponing for each item you toss. Out with that moldy package of cream cheese; in with calling that friend you've never called back. Toss that nasty jar of mayonnaise from 2002; replace it with that long-postponed trip to wine country (where you can restock your vintage bottle of wine). Unworn clothes go to Goodwill – the knit sweater your aunt crocheted that you never wore; go take that foreign language course. Remember when you wanted to learn French? *Oui?* Treat yourself to an adventure.

Don't wait.

Expiration date: Today.

X

XANADU.
"A place where nobody dared to go . . .
The love that we came to know . . . They call it Xanadu."

*"*A*nd now*
Open your eyes and see
What we have made is real

We are in Xanadu . . ."[35]

With lyrics like that, who wouldn't want to go there? *Plus* it's a romantic musical fantasy film. *Plus* it stars the ever-glamorous Olivia Newton-John *and* she wears roller skates *and* the trailer for this 1980 adventure dares us to "Open your eyes and hear the magic!"[36]

I mean, come on!

So here's the plot. Sonny Malone is a talented artist (sound familiar?) who dreams of fame (sound familiar?) who's on the verge of giving up on his dream (sound familiar?) when he collides with a girl on roller skates (and why not?) only to lose her, obsess about her (sound familiar?), then find her again! But he can't have her because . . . wait for it . . . she's a Mt. Olympus Greek goddess muse. (Then there's this whole other subplot about a nightclub opening with Gene Kelly as an orchestra leader, Zeus and a magical mural, and this whole animated sequence set to the Electric Light Orchestra song, "Don't Walk Away", that looks like a forerunner to *Aladdin*, and . . . Holy shit! Why don't they make movies like this anymore?)

So what's the point? Well, the tagline for the movie is, "Xanadu. The story of a girl who makes dreams come true."[37]

Just like Sonny Malone, we all have dreams. But since most of us don't have a roller-skating hottie named Kira who's a descendant of the Olympian Gods to make them come true, we've got to do the work ourselves.

Dammit! I want Kira!

But what if we've never really been taught how to go about doing that?

Have we ever stopped and wondered . . . What makes things happen? What makes someone else book a job while we constantly get passed over? What makes someone else land a perfect girlfriend while we continue to stay single? Why does everything happen to them, but not to us?

Well, let's talk science again, because it's fun!

As we know, atoms are the basic building blocks of everything in the universe. They come together (or actually are repelled), and in so doing, form mass. You. Me. A chair. A Pop Tart. A unicorn. A Hershey's Kiss. A roller rink. Atomically speaking, it's all the same. And though atoms collectively form material, they are individually made up of 99.9% empty space.

Now, if our bodies are made up entirely of atoms, then you and I and our friends and lovers and moms and dads and everyone on the planet are all 99.9% space. And we're also energy and electricity, which makes us like Kira . . . *cosmic.*

Space is immeasurable. It's infinite. It's expansive.

Scientifically, then, *we* are infinite. We are infinite space.

We have a hard time connecting to that truth because we're stuck on the physical form of matter. We look at ourselves and see things we don't like. Our nose is too big; our lips are too small. We don't look like Heidi Klum. Our skin sags at the elbow, we have dark circles under our eyes, we're losing our hair.

We look at our world and see things that aren't happening for us. We see the lack of support, or no boyfriend, a career that seems to be stalled, the inability to catch a break or cash a check because we don't have enough funds in our account.

If we continue to view our life only from the materialistic viewpoint (that of matter), it's very difficult to create change. That's because, from a quantum perspective, the level of transformation we're looking for doesn't occur in the material world. It occurs at the quantum level (the energy level).

So, part of shifting our paradigms to create new experiences in our lives requires that we make changes at that level.

We can't get stuck on how something looks. We want to introduce new pictures through our intention *before* these thoughts actually move from the world of possibility to the world of matter.

Part of what keeps us from creating more vibrantly in our lives is that there is a part of us that remains skeptical. Cynical. Doubting. Part of restructuring our paradigms requires us to do a thorough investigation of the things we've been taught to believe and examine *why* we believe them in the first place. And in so doing, you may begin to ask yourself, "What do I have to lose in looking at my life from a new perspective?"

Nothing.

Except maybe letting go of all the things that seem to hold you back. And that doesn't seem like a loss to me at all.

And what might you gain? Well, *Xanadu*, of course.

As you become more mindful of how you create, you begin to see that the answers lie deep within us. Or, as Olivia sang in her chart-topping *Xanadu* hit, "Magic":

Come take my hand
You should know me
I've always been in your mind
You know I will be kind
I'll be guiding you

Building your dream
Has to start now
There's no other road to take
You won't make a mistake
I'll be guiding you

You have to believe we are magic
Nothin' can stand in our way

You have to believe we are magic
Don't let your aim ever stray

And if all your hopes survive
Destiny will arrive
I'll bring all your dreams alive
For you[38]

Y

WHY?

Probing into Life's questions helps us to discover
a spiritual foundation we're all meant to uncover.

In one of his stand-up shows, comedian Louis C.K. hilariously recounts a conversation he had with his daughter. It started innocently enough when she asked why she couldn't go outside and Mr. C.K. replied, "Because it's raining." His daughter then asked, "Why?" "Well, water's coming out of the sky." "Why?" "Because it was in a cloud." "Why?" She kept asking that million-dollar question for the next 45 minutes . . . *"Why?"* . . . in response to *everything* he said to her. "Well clouds form when there's vapor!" "Why?" "I don't know! I don't know any more things! Those are all the things I know!" "Why?"[39] On and on, she took him (as I'm sure all parents are taken by their kids' questions) down a wormhole of exasperations, head explosions, migraines, cosmic Big Bang theories, existentialism, and the meaning of it all.

Children have this innate curiosity that forces them to keep asking questions about the world they're living in. Partly because they're like this blank computer chip waiting to be filled with information, but also because they possess an innate desire to know.

Somewhere along the line, as we get older — and supposedly "wiser" — we often stop asking these kinds of penetrating questions, because, well, who wants to face *those* truths? I'd much rather ask, "Do you make skinny margaritas on the rocks with Splenda?"

An active inquiry into ourselves requires us to be conscious and *here* — emotionally available and willing to look at our hidden fears. It forces us to be honest in areas we may not want to examine that closely. By engaging in a conscious examination of the questions we ask ourselves and continuing to probe deeper into where they come from, we begin to uncover the root of many of our challenges. Like, "Why do I hold these beliefs and where do they come from?" "Why do I settle for second best?" "Why do I think in terms of limitation and defeat?"

We may uncover locked doors of low self-esteem and anemic self-love that have been left unexamined but are still festering and poisonous. We may unravel our relationship with self-worth and realize how much or how little we actually value ourselves.

Staying in an active dialogue with ourselves about things that want to take us deeper than the more superficial questions we often ask ("Why did Selena break up with the Biebs?") opens us to spiritual discoveries of our core being.

I remember at the beginning of my spiritual journey, when I first learned to meditate (and even after one of my first trips to India), I struggled with questions of faith. I thought I'd wake up one day and all my doubts and insecurities would be gone because I was on a "path."

They weren't. In fact, they got louder.

Who was I to think I was spiritual?

Years later, I read an autobiography of the spiritual icon and Nobel Prize winner, Mother Teresa. It was a watershed moment. The woman who had been publicly portrayed as the most saintly and devout of nuns actually had many dissonant feelings about her faith. She struggled and felt alone and lost. She said she was hypocritical because the outward face presented to the world was smiling and beatific, but inwardly, she often experienced absolute confusion and disbelief. Who'd have thought that the woman who was considered the most faithful woman in the world actually struggled bitterly with her faith?

The moral of this story is twofold. First and foremost, we mustn't let contradicting thoughts inhibit our exploration and expansion into ourselves or derail us from our life's path. Mother Teresa was even more a hero because, in spite of her contrary thoughts, she continued to do such serviceable work (especially hard to do in those very constricting nun habits made out of polyester!). Even though she didn't wear breathable fabric, she helped millions. Her inner battles didn't leave her inert or feeling sorry for herself.

"God, I just can't possibly wear blue and white again today, please!"

Second, even if and when our path takes us down dark and intimidating roads, we need to continue forward. Mother Teresa kept engaging in a deep exploration of "Why?" throughout her journey even if it led her down paths of confusion, sadness, loss of hope, and faithlessness.

That's called being a spiritual bad-ass warrior.

Spirituality isn't intended for us to become all *"Rama-Lama Ding-Dong"* about it, and float up to the stratosphere and disconnect from our responsibilities by always having a spiritual excuse or explanation for things and use words we would *never* (!) use in a sentence (like *astral dimensions, physical plane, auras*). It's not about making this world less important than "other" worlds or avoiding feeling that is painful because we think it's "an illusion."

It's not about looking and sounding like an "enlightened" person saying all the right things but really using that as a veil or a wall to mask or disconnect or hide from what's really going on inside.

A spiritual awakening — realizing our own warrior spirit — asks us to step out into the world and stay in it, leading from the heart. Leading from compassion and patience and grace. *That requires guts.* Fortitude. Equanimity. A sense of humor. Humility. And dogged determination.

To ferret out the truth of *your being* is hard work. The path is narrow and steep and full of pitfalls. And it's lonely. I can't call up Deepak or Oprah or Eckhart or Gaga and have them go with me. Oh, crap. It must be walked alone. All of us in life will — at one point or another — have a calling to follow this path and heed its teachings. Some go. Some don't. But once we decide to walk it, there's no turning back. We're met with darkness and fears and shattering of illusions, and as Joseph Campbell says, we take our own "hero's journey."[40]

And that takes real spiritual *balls.*

Actually, it just takes balls. Period.

And that's really why we're all here. To meet, face-to-face, our own Self.

It's often said that living a truly spiritual life is like walking on a double-edged sword. It always cuts with one side or another; so walking it is a very delicate, balanced, nuanced *awareness* each step of the way.

Why?

Because it can cut you deeply.

Why?

Because drawing blood is painful.

Why?

Because it makes you look at the things an open wound reveals to you.

Why?

Because it's actually opened in order to be fully healed.

Why?

Because in healing, we discover our real sense of Self. We aren't our wounds.

Why?

Because it was intended this way. And each step we take brings us closer to this realization: The true hero in life is our own hero within. Fully capable, knowledgeable and already whole.

So keep asking "Why?" and you'll get there.

Z

ZYMURGY.

Your life is this laboratory – like brewing a beer.
Once you discover your Self, there's nothing to fear.

When I was in 10th grade chemistry class I found the idea of Bunsen burners and experiments, test tubes and explosions, so sexy. Who wouldn't? Standing there in a polyester white lab coat with black-rimmed glasses, pouring nitrous oxide into a glass container and watching it smoke as I tried to make out the image of star quarterback, Todd McMillan, through the sulphuric haze made it all seem so *Weird Science*.

But then, reality set in. Having to take tests on chemical equations (that scarily seemed more like trigonometry theorems) made me get out of that class faster than you can say "Lord Voldemort."

I ended up taking a P.E. elective instead. And continued dreaming of Todd while I learned how to properly square dance and double-dutch jump rope. (Two skills that come in handy still today.) But now I regret my days of failed chemistry experimentation. Why?

Because life itself *is* chemistry. It is the science of *matter* after all, but it's also about the atomic nature of things interacting and *transforming*. We are attracted to people and things; turned on, turned off, repelled, excited — all because of the chemical reactions that occur within us in relationship to pretty much everything.

The modern study of chemistry has its genesis in the ancient tradition of *alchemy*, which is the transmutation of base metals into gold. Dating back to ancient Egypt (around 1900 B.C.) and then China and India (2nd to 5th century A.D.), spiritual alchemy has been known as the art and science of liberating parts of us from this temporal experience into the truths of who we are beyond the physical.

With me so far? I told you it was a little like chem class.

Well, for all us White Zinfandel, Chablis-lovin', wine cooler-drinking partiers — or the beer-kegger in us all — we've already got a head start on this alchemy thing. Zymurgy is the branch of chemistry involved in making wine or brewing beer. Basically, we're like a glass of fine wine. And not that cheap-ass Two-Buck Chuck from Trader Joe's. I'm talking vintage stuff here.

But like wine, some things take years to fully blossom into a beautiful, aromatic bouquet. Which means, the process of our life's unfolding is alchemical. It's a process of creating and trying things and experimenting and attempting. It's going to take awhile to get it right. And it requires a constant participation in the mixing and stirring, measuring and pouring. Otherwise, it's going to just stagnate and get really gross and ferment . . . like vinegar.

Don't let your life spoil.

You are the scientist *and* the experiment. You can't be scared to get your hands dirty. The wonderful thing about alchemy is that it's always a work in progress. There's no getting it wrong. It's just trial and error. Step and repeat. Hit and miss. The macro sits in the micro. The failures generate the successes. All of them. And *all* moments of the entire history of the universe have led us to this exact moment in time. Now.

Holy crap. Can we get our heads around that? *All* moments have led us to this moment *right now*. So stay in the alchemy.

Isaac Newton, whose scientific mechanics transformed physics and our understanding of universal laws, remained a life-long *alchemist*. (Although he died a virgin at the age of 85, so perhaps he might have tried a little more *experimentation!*)

Our journey is an ever-evolving, perpetual art form. And *we* are the art. In order to make art, we have to experiment. Experimentation is the key. We wouldn't be where we are today without it. Half the time we're doing it unconsciously anyway.

But what would happen if we tried to be a bit more conscious? Perhaps we'd be like those great inventors, those Nobel laureates, those Peace Prize winners and visionary discoverers.

What we might uncover is the most brilliant discovery we could ever find: Ourselves.

What quantum physics, science, and alchemy tell us — and what we're here to remember — is that life isn't merely about discovering reality. It's about creating it.

So create it the way you want it to be: a chemical equation of love and passion and hope and possibility and enthusiasm and joy and truth.

Everything we already are.

From A to Z.

ACKNOWLEDGEMENTS

I have many people to thank, without whose stellar support
and guidance and reality checks I wouldn't have a book.

E is for Editor, Sharon Blynn,
who has the insight, patience, and beauty of a modern-day Kuan Yin.

S is for Steve Bermundo, whose illustrations are fantastical.
Irreverent and insightful, they make this book's world — I think — quite magical.

E is for Eric, an assistant whose intelligence outweighs his charm.
A man I truly trust and who keeps me from harm.

R is for Robin, the Minister of Information.
She can change the tire on a jumbo jet
while giving someone mouth-to-mouth resuscitation.
I'm grateful beyond exaggeration.

B is for Becca, who fact-checked beyond being a nerd.
Her dedication and commitment is, well, inspiringly absurd.

T is for Tyler, I call him Tippecanoe. Not for its well-known history,
but because his ability to quote lines from obscure movies is an utter mystery.

S is for Sean, Master Teacher and Friend.
He toiled with this title until we got to the end:
Alphabet Soup for Grown-Ups — a helping hand he did lend.

B is for Barbara, or Babs as she is known.
Enthusiastic, excited, gleeful — she'll leave you all that (and then some) after the tone.

A is for All the Students I've ever taught, who continue to expand an ever-evolving teaching.
You inspire me to go higher and keep on reaching.

T is for the Teachers who bless me — and our studios — with service and support.
Without you this work would not have progressed past Broadway and West 4th.

E is for Elise. Thanks for your supportive set of eyes.
Ummm . . . all you single men out there need to wake up, because she's totally a prize.

N is for Nancy — a brilliant artist who doesn't yet know.
What she has to contribute to the world is a Light that can supremely glow.

K is for Mr. Kent, my dearest friend and truly a gent.
His guidance and support of all things AMAW is 100%.

L is for Laura, an artist most graphic.
Her skills on computer programs are of those that could stop traffic.

J is for Jonah, a true writing whiz.
His support and insight has helped me to navigate this Biz.

R is for the Readers who've opened me to a whole new world.
I'm grateful for your readership and the inspiration it unfurls.

SELECT BIBLIOGRAPHY

[1] Gorey, Edward. *The Gashlycrumb Tinies*. Orlando, FL: Harcourt Books. 1963. Print.

[2] Dery, Mark. "Edward Gorey's Gothic Tales From the Vault." *Los Angeles Times*. October 26, 2012. Newspaper. Retrieved from: http://articles.latimes.com/2012/oct/26/entertainment/la-ca-jc-edward-gorey-20121028

[3] *The Quantum Activist*. Dir. Renee Slade & Ri Stewart. Intention Media. 2009. Film.
Full Quote: "In between doing, what happens? The possibilities grow. And grow and grow and grow. Possibilities are different. Now anybody knows if there are more possibilities to choose from, my chance of choosing the correct possibility that will answer my problem is better. Isn't that true?"

[4] *Notes on a Scandal*. Dir. Richard Eyre. Fox Searchlight Pictures. 2006. Film.

[5] *The Quantum Activist*. Dir. Renee Slade & Ri Stewart. Intention Media. 2009. Film.

[6] Mook, David & Raleigh, Ben. *Scooby-Doo* Theme Song.

[7] *Bridalplasty*. E! Entertainment. 2010. Television.

[8] *Mean Girls*. Dir. Mark Waters. Paramount Pictures. 2004. Film.

[9] 57th Annual Academy Awards. ABC. March 25, 1985. Television.

[10] O'Connor, Maureen. "All the Terrible Things Mel Gibson Has Said on the Record." *Gawker.com*. Gawker Media. July 8, 2010. Web. August 14, 2012.

[11] 25th Miss Teen USA Pageant. NBC. August 24, 2007. Television.

[12] 25th Miss Teen USA Pageant. NBC. August 24, 2007. Television.

[13] *The Undersea World of Jacques Cousteau*. A&E. 1968–1974. Television.

[14] Frank, Adam. *About Time: Cosmology and Culture at the Twilight of the Big Bang*. New York, NY: Simon and Schuster. 2011. Print.

[15] McBride, Joseph. *Steven Spielberg: A Biography*. New York, NY: Simon and Schuster. 2010. Print.

[16] Mitchell, Elvis. "Joaquin Phoenix." *Interview*. October 17, 2012. Magazine. Retrieved from: http://www.interviewmagazine.com/film/joaquin-phoenix#_

[17] Cieply, Michael. "What Makes Spielberg Jump?" *New York Times*. October 28, 2011. MT1. Newspaper.

[18] Achor, Shawn. *The Happiness Advantage: The Seven Principles of Positive Psychology That Fuel Success and Performance at Work*. New York, NY: Crown Business. 2010. Print.

[19] Williamson, Marianne. Teachings Based on *A Course in Miracles* Weekly in Los Angeles. Los Angeles. The Saban Theatre. Monday, December 3, 2012. Lecture.

[20] Chödrön, Pema. *The Wisdom of No Escape and the Path of Loving Kindness*. Boston, MA: Shambhala Publications, Inc. 1991. Print.

[21] Walker, Thomas. *The Force Is With Us: The Higher Consciousness That Science Refuses to Accept*. Wheaton, IL: Quest Books. 2009. Print.

[22] Chopra, Deepak (DeepakChopra). "Thoughts are probability waves from the conditioned mind that shape everyday reality. True creativity comes from pure consciousness." August 19, 2012, 6:42 AM. Tweet.

[23] Maslow, A.H. "A Theory of Human Motivation." *Psychological Review*. 1943. Page 383. Magazine. Retrieved from: http://psychclassics.yorku.ca/Maslow/motivation.htm.

[24] "Ira Glass on Storytelling". Current TV. Web Video. http://www.thisamericanlife.org/about/make-radio.

[25] Think Progress TP. "Elizabeth Warren Explains: 'No, Governor Romney, Corporations Are Not People.'" Online video clip. *YouTube*. YouTube, September 5, 2012. Web. September 6, 2012.

[26] Frank, Adam. *About Time: Cosmology and Culture at the Twilight of the Big Bang.* New York, NY: Simon and Schuster. 2011. Print.

[27] Lanza, Robert. *Biocentrism: How Life and Consciousness Are the Keys to Understanding the True Nature of the Universe.* Dallas, TX: BenBella Books, Inc. 2009. Print.

[28] Lanza, Robert. *Biocentrism: How Life and Consciousness Are the Keys to Understanding the True Nature of the Universe.* Dallas, TX: BenBella Books, Inc. 2009. Print.

[29] Lanza, Robert. *Biocentrism: How Life and Consciousness Are the Keys to Understanding the True Nature of the Universe.* Dallas, TX: BenBella Books, Inc. 2009. Print.

[30] Stanner, W. E. H. *The Dreaming & Other Essays.* Collingwood VIC: Black Inc. Agenda. 2009. Print.

[31] Calaprice, Alice. *The Ultimate Quotable Einstein.* Princeton, NJ: Princeton University Press. 2011. Print.

[32] Pilon, Mary. "The 400: Aching to Win." *New York Times.* July 8, 2012. SP1. Newspaper.

[33] Abramowitz, Rachel. "Riffs on Life, In the Key of Jack." *Los Angeles Times.* November 3, 2002. Newspaper. Retrieved from: http://www.nytimes.com/2008/10/02/health/nutrition/02best.html?_r=0

[34] Alexander, Larry. "Life Is Being on the Wire. Everything Else Is Just Waiting." LancasterOnline.com. Lancaster Newspapers. May 25, 2007. Web. October 15, 2012.

[35] *Xanadu.* Dir. Robert Greenwald. Universal Pictures. 1980. Film.

[36] "Xanadu." *The Internet Movie Database.* IMDb.com, Inc, 1990-2013. http://www.imdb.com/video/screenplay/vi3923902745/

[37] "Xanadu." *The Internet Movie Database.* IMDb.com, Inc, 1990-2013. http://www.imdb.com/title/tt0081777/

[38] *Xanadu.* Dir. Robert Greenwald. Universal Pictures. 1980. Film.

[39] AmmonRa801. "Louis C.K. 'Why?'" Online video clip. *YouTube.* YouTube, May 5, 2007. Web. November 8, 2012.

[40] Campbell, Joseph. *The Hero's Journey: Joseph Campbell on His Life and Work.* Novato, California: New World Library. 2003. Print.

ABOUT THE AUTHOR

Anthony Meindl is an award-winning writer, director, producer and Artistic Director of Anthony Meindl's Actor Workshop in Los Angeles, where it's been named the #1 Acting School by *Backstage* Magazine. He also has schools in New York, London, and Vancouver, and travels internationally to teach his revolutionary creative work to people from all walks of life.

As a writer/producer/director/actor, Meindl's first feature film, *Birds of a Feather*, won the Spirit of the Festival Award at the 2012 Honolulu Rainbow Film Festival and he won Best Director at the Downtown Film Festival Los Angeles. It is being released on DVD/itunes/VOD and theatrically in March 2014. He is a regular contributor to *The Daily Love, The Huffington Post, Backstage,* and various spiritual magazines and podcasts. He's been featured on ABC News and KTLA, and in *The Advocate* and *The Hollywood Reporter,* among others, and was a keynote speaker at the 2013 Global Alliance for Transformation in Entertainment Conference, co-founded by Jim Carrey and Eckhart Tolle. Meindl's first book, *At Left Brain Turn Right,* released last year, has helped artists of all kinds unleash their creative genius within. And his YouTube page has become a popular destination for people wanting to find an irreverent and practical understanding of spirituality and creative potential.

He lives in Los Angeles.

Follow him on Twitter @AnthonyMeindl

ABOUT THE ILLUSTRATOR

Steve Bermundo was born in the Philippines and now resides in Los Angeles where he makes his living as both an illustrator and as a professional dancer.

Mr. Bermundo has always had a love for drawing and illustrations. Throughout his elementary and high school years, he excelled in the visual arts. It was in high school that he also discovered his talent in the performing arts and has been living as a professional dancer in Los Angeles for over 20 years. He now juggles his time between the stage and the drawing board. In addition to *Alphabet Soup for Grown- Ups*, he has also illustrated several childrens' books.

You can find more of his illustrations at www.BearMoonDoe.com